What Readers And Reviewers Are Saying About This Book

"Mind-Blowing... Clearly, one of the most valuable persuasion books I have ever experienced.

From the moment I picked it up, I didn't want to put it down. I'm giving copies of this book to my entire team.

This should be required reading for anyone in business. Frankly, if you're trying to impress or sell anyone and you don't know this, I believe you may have a massive disadvantage,"

--Jack Canfield, Coauthor of the Chicken Soup for the Soul® Series

"One of the most important marketing books I have ever experienced."

--Mike Scotto, Former Division Director of Marketing, JCPenney, SCORE National Advisory Council

****BOOKLIFE PRIZE** WINNER**

"With the scope of a textbook and the intimacy of a trusted advisor, this book... is a must-read for anyone who wants their message to be unforgettable.

An easy-to-read and entertaining guide packed with strategies for taking sales to the next level."

--*Critic's Report – The BookLife Prize*

****READERS' FAVORITE 5-STAR AWARD WINNER****

"This book is terrific.

It lives up to its promise and more. I could hardly put the book down after I started reading it.

I [especially] liked the interactive nature of the book; getting involved helps readers apply the principles that they're learning.

Best of all, most of the ideas Bond presents are simple and virtually cost-free.

I highly recommend this superb marketing book to anyone who wants to increase their product or service's visibility and make more sales. I'm applying some of what I learned to my own marketing efforts."

--*Reviewer Joe Wisinski for Readers' Favorite Awards*

****EDITOR'S PICK** FROM PUBLISHERS WEEKLY**

"Strategy-packed...

This book showcases how making something "stick" in a potential buyer's memory greatly increases the likelihood of creating an actual buyer."

--*Booklife for Publishers Weekly*

FIVE-STAR READER REVIEWS

Do Not Read This - Without a Highlighter Handy!

"I was not prepared for how many real-life scenarios this book had.

Excellent read! Cannot recommend this book highly enough."

--Mandy Westover

Brain Glue - Gets Your Message to Stick

"A confused prospect won't buy. Unclear marketing messages don't sell.

This book gives you the easy button for creating marketing messages that stick in your prospects' mind and gets them to buy."

--Bill Brelsford

Essential... Even For Experienced Marketers

"I was only a couple of pages in, and I already have a TON of new ideas to market my business and new service offering.

I highly recommend you buy this book, even if you've been in marketing for years (as I have been!)

--Dr. Sandi Eveleth

Textbook On Being "Persuasive"

"This should be a textbook required for all marketing classes.

It's making me rethink how I sell, so I'm more persuasive. Definitely interesting."

--Amazon Customer

You Had Me at Half Assed (Refers to the Book's Previous Title)

"James has found a way to take what we know about old school marketing, and actually communicates WHY it works, and how to apply it to today's markets, in a way that is both informative and entertaining!

I will be making this required reading for All my Mentoring clients."

--*Stephanie E*

Excellent Book – Explains Why Certain Brands Explode

"Ever wondered why some brands suddenly explode? Wonder no more! This book contains some mind-blowing strategies that you can use in your everyday marketing which will definitely help your business stand out from the crowd. Up to date and well researched with plenty of information you can implement today."

--*Amazon Reader*

AUDIBLE 5-STAR REVIEWS

A Must-Buy

"Having an MBA and working in corporate for a long time, including in advertising and sales, I have read a lot of books about business, communication, sales, writing, and influence.

This book has ideas I have not seen before, and they're brilliant.

Books on these topics can be quite dry, but this is a radiant exception. It was hard for me to put it down because the storytelling and the narration are so compelling.

If you apply even 10% of the suggestions and evidence-based wisdom contained in this book, you will see a radical difference in the way you show up in business and in any area of your life in which you are looking to be noticed and influential.

Don't sleep on this—this book is likely to be on "top business book" lists for years to come."

--Jayme C

The Most Persuasive Book Ever

"This is the type of book that has the power to change my business, my attitude, my productiveness, and ultimately, my life.

I'm in the process of preparing a TV show to pitch, so I feel completely blessed to have come across this book at the perfect time. The author touches on how these principles are also applied to the entertainment industry, including pitching a television project!

The power of persuasion can work in every aspect of your life. Once this is mastered, the things we can manifest and accomplish are as abundant as the drops of water on the shores of the beautiful Pacific Ocean. ;-) (I'm learning !) 8 thumbs up from [everyone in] my household!!!"

--MakedaTene

I'm a Fan

"As a new entrepreneur starting to launch my medical spa, this book had me rethinking my whole marketing process, from renaming my products to changing my slogan.

YES!!! It was that powerful.

Bond described 14 persuasion triggers that will ignite your clients "buying brain" in ways you didn't know existed.

The author used his marketing background to simplify the subject, and without a doubt, grabbed the reader's attention. It was captivating, interesting, educational, and career-changing to say the least. Well done!!!"

--Wildangel

Brain Glue™

How Selling Becomes Much Easier By Making Your Ideas "Sticky"

James I. Bond

Published by U.S. Management, LLC, Thousand Oaks, California.
Previously published under the titles – Sell More With A Right-Brain Marketing Strategy, and, Dump Your Half-Assed Marketing Strategy

ISBN: 978-0-9988657-4-4 (Hardback) ISBN: 978-0-9988657-5-1 (Paperback)

Yes, This Book's Title Was Changed

This book was previously published as: "Sell More With A Right-Brain Marketing Strategy," but the title BRAIN GLUE made more sense, because that's the subject of the book.

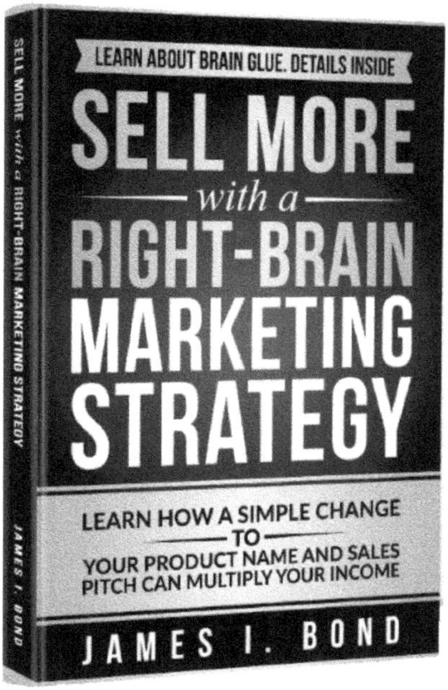

I changed the title when just about everyone told me the title BRAIN GLUE makes more sense. LOL. So yes, I do listen to you, the audience! Thanks to everyone for your awesome feedback!

If you enjoy this book...

Please Leave a 1-Click Review

(It makes a huge difference!)

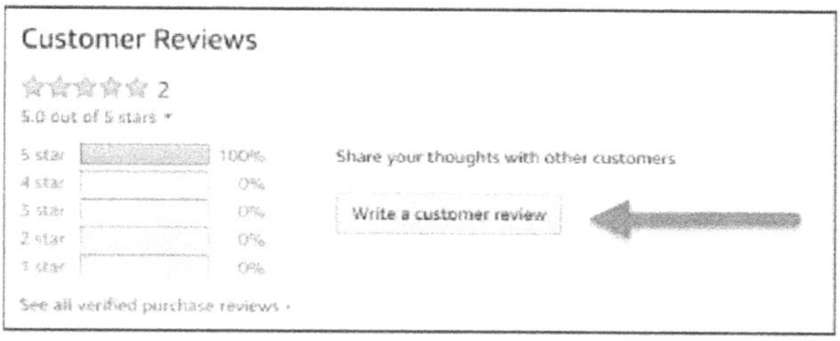

If you enjoy this book,
I would be incredibly thankful if you take just 60 seconds to write a brief review on Amazon,
even if it's just a few sentences.

Thank you!

Contents

How BRAIN GLUE™ Makes Your Ideas "Sticky" So They Stick to Your Prospect's Brain Like Glue

The Secret To Accelerated Persuasion

In the pages that follow, you are about to discover the behavioral power that BRAIN GLUE has to influence, persuade, and sell just about anyone, anywhere, anytime.

Through fourteen specific strategies, BRAIN GLUE amplifies the persuasive power of your ads, social media posts, emails, and face-to-face presentations – in many cases beating major brands and wealthy competitors – by transforming simple phrases into blockbusters of persuasion.

Introduction

Why a Right-Brain Marketing Strategy Can Be So Valuable

What if a simple change in the words you use could amplify your ability to influence, persuade and sell just about anyone, anytime, anyplace?

What if slightly altering the name of your product, the title of your book, or the description of your idea, could make it easier to get people saying YES to you?

Welcome to BRAIN GLUE, the secret power tool of the most advanced marketing and persuasion experts. Once you start to understand the impact of right-brain selling through the behavioral tools of BRAIN GLUE, you'll wonder why no one told you about this before.

As one of America's leading behavioral management specialists, I'm about to expose you to a few simple techniques and strategies that only top marketers, attorneys, and politicians know how to use, to turn even their most moderate ideas, pitches, and products into winners.

This is a marketing strategy made simple by using advanced behavioral management tools.

It's something these top marketers, attorneys, and politicians don't want you to know for fear their competitors will begin to discover the power of this and start using it against them.

But in the pages that follow, I'll share it with you, right here, right now. Once you begin to learn this, I believe everything will change for you.

Are you ready?

As actress Bette Davis said in the movie, All About Eve, *"Fasten your seatbelts; it's going to be a bumpy night!"*

My Four-Year-Old Daughter Didn't Want To Have Sex With The Boy Next Door

When she was four years old, I remember our middle daughter, Lauren, standing with a few friends outside our home when one of the kids asked if she liked Allen, the boy next door.

Lauren's response, *"I like him, but I don't want to have sex with him."*

Yikes! As a parent, what do you say to your daughter when she says something like that?

I looked around for my wife, but she was nowhere to be found. So, it was up to me to intervene somehow.

I've often asked this question in the marketing and behavioral management classes I've conducted at two major universities and through my workshops with the U.S. Small Business Administration.

Many of my students respond with shock that a little girl would say such a thing.

But then, they hear the punchline.

I asked Lauren, *"What's sex?"*

"That's kissing."

"Yup," I responded. *"Don't do that; you'll get germs."*

Then I quickly escaped.

The point of this is somewhat profound. Why would we think a four-year-old has the same understanding of what sex is that we do? Yet universally, we tend to believe others have the same understanding as we do about what we're offering or proposing when often that's not the case at all.

Think about it.

If we get it wrong with a four-year-old, how often do we get it wrong with our peers and prospects?

We believe people understand what we are proposing and what we are offering. But what if their understanding is nowhere near what we expect? What if our prospect or listener is missing something critical to their making the right decision, and we don't even realize it?

This is an issue I've addressed for over three decades with thousands of clients and students. Do our prospects truly understand what we're offering? Or are we fooling ourselves by asking them to buy our products and ideas based on their misunderstanding of what's being offered or proposed, making it almost impossible for them to say yes to us?

For droves of the clients and students I've worked with, all it took was a slight change in the behavioral strategy they used to dramatically increase the number and quality of people who said YES to their products and ideas.

It's enough to make us wonder if solving this lack of clarity over what you are offering – by introducing what could be among the most potent behavioral tools that exists – whether that could open your floodgates of persuasion so wide that it suddenly becomes significantly easier to reach your goals, even your personal ones?

I believe the answer is YES, and that's what I'll be exploring with you in the pages that follow.

Like the thousands of students who have attended my breakthrough sessions, I believe you are about to discover behavioral tools that will open your mind to the kinds of results you crave on a level you've never experienced before.

Gaining A Communication Edge

Let's begin with this.

What's the most powerful tool of human interaction that exists? I'm using it now, aren't I? Can you tell what I'm doing? What am I doing?

That's right. I'm using questions. Questions are the most powerful tool of human interaction that exists, aren't they? When you hear a question, you instinctively want to answer it, don't you? It's a reflex built into us.

But...

What if there's a question or phrase you could use that's so powerful, it makes people want to buy from you even before they hear or read your entire pitch? Would that simplify your ability to influence, persuade and sell just about anyone?

Absolutely, and in ways that may surprise you.

Before we get into that, let's explore why questions trigger an automatic interaction in us, in the first place.

The secret lies with something that's wired into our brains called redintegration. Not re-integration, but redintegration.

Redintegration is the brain's need for completion. For example, when we hear HALF a story, a trigger goes off inside our brain that expects the second half.

Redintegration is why we watch crappy movies and tv shows to the end, even when we know the show is stupid. Once a problem is introduced, we need to watch it to the end to see how it gets resolved.

Redintegration is why we like symmetry. But it's also why unbalanced and asymmetric things grab our attention.

Take the joke, *"fool me once, shame on you; fool me twice... congratulations."*

For most of us, once we heard the beginning of this phrase, *"Fool me once, shame on you..."* we expected the second part, *"Fool me twice, shame on me."* By twisting the ending, we get a memorable surprise that resonates with most listeners.

Actually, there are two psychological elements at play here.

One is the fact that our brains are already programmed to recognize specific phrases and patterns. So, anchoring our product or idea to something already 'stuck' inside our listener's brain will also trigger an additional part of their brain – the same region where images are processed, and decisions are made.

A brilliant example of this is when Procter & Gamble introduced a dandruff shampoo in 1961. They knew that most Americans had learned the children's rhyme,

"Head and shoulders, knees and toes... eyes, ears, mouth, and nose."

By capitalizing on something that was already 'stuck' in almost everyone's brain, they realized that naming their shampoo *'Head & Shoulders'* would help make it an instant hit because the name would already feel familiar, and because using that phrase would trigger positive emotions in almost everyone who heard it.

And they were right, as Head & Shoulders continues to be hugely successful more than sixty years after it was initially launched.

But the reverse is also true.

We could start with a pattern that's already inside a person's brain and grab their attention by introducing a surprise ending, as was done with the *"fool me twice"* example I just mentioned.

Why Should You Care About Any Of This

Not knowing this will give you a massive disadvantage if you want to influence, persuade, and sell easier and faster than you're doing it now.

Consider this...

How would your life change if persuasion suddenly became much easier for you? If your conversations, social media posts, presentations, emails, and ads were suddenly more effective at getting people to agree with you and buy from you?

Understanding patterns in how our brains work and using those patterns to make it easier for people to accept our ideas and buy our products is what you're about to learn in the pages that follow.

Whether you're a creative person trying to sell your idea, a marketer trying to get people to buy your product, an attorney trying to convince a jury that your client is innocent, a politician trying to persuade the masses of something you feel is essential, or even a single person trying to get a date with the love of your life, this could be one of the most important strategies you learn.

Consider this.

What does the phrase, *"If the glove don't fit, you must acquit,"* and the product named *'Squatty Potty'* have in common?

More than you probably realize.

Each of these phrases has helped achieve unexpectedly high breakthrough successes by activating the emotion centers of their audience's brains – the exact place where decisions are made.

In the murder trial of celebrity OJ Simpson, attorney Johnnie Cochran used the phrase,

"If the glove don't fit, you must acquit."

Another attorney might have said,

"If the glove doesn't fit my client, you have to let him go free."

But phrasing it with rhyme and street-talk made it instrumental in almost miraculously convincing a jury to let his client go free, despite overwhelming evidence against him. He triggered their emotions, and that often overrides logic.

When asked why they found OJ not guilty, at least two of the jurors explained, *"We knew, if the glove don't fit, we must acquit. The glove didn't fit, so we had to acquit."*

Then there's the product named *'Squatty Potty.'* This simple toilet stool generated more than $100 million dollars of sales in less than two years. In a large part, it accomplished this because of its almost humorous name.

What if the product was called *'The Toilet Stool?'* Do you believe sales would have exploded as they did?

Of course not.

Each of these phrases achieved outstanding success by using something I call BRAIN GLUE.

Like the trigger that turned Head & Shoulders into a massive success, BRAIN GLUE gets your audience's brain activated by making your idea, product name, book title, or attempt at persuasion 'sticky,' so it sticks in your prospect's brain like glue. Once your idea is stuck in your prospect's brain, getting them to buy can become infinitely easier.

In fact, many of the world's top Attorneys, Politicians, Salespeople, Advertisers, and even Comedians have discovered this secret... that right-brain emotion-activating words, phrases, and patterns have a more remarkable ability to influence, persuade and sell just about anyone than the logic-filled presentations and arguments so many of us have been trained to make since grade school.

After all, people buy mostly for emotional reasons. Yet, even early in our schooling, we've been taught to present almost exclusively using logical arguments.

That's nuts!

Consider some of the most influential and funny phrases that have been used over the years.

Like this...

"Don't sweat the petty things... or pet the sweaty things."

This was a joke from famed comedian George Carlin, who often used BRAIN GLUE-type techniques to generate laughs with his often-provocative observations about life.

Or, if you're old enough to remember this advertising slogan, how about this...

"It takes a licking... and keeps on ticking."

In one of the classes I conducted for the U.S. Small Business Administration, I started this phrase, *"It takes a licking..."* and just about everyone over forty completed it. When I asked who it was an ad for, without hesitation they said Timex Watches.

What's so amazing about this?

The last time an ad with this slogan ran was more than twenty-five years ago. Yet, people remembered it like it was yesterday.

That's the power of BRAIN GLUE.

How about this...

"Ask not what your country can do for you.
Ask what you can do for your country."

U.S. President John F. Kennedy often created iconic quotes like this that encouraged patriotism and volunteerism throughout America, using a classic BRAIN GLUE technique called 'chiasmus.'

Do you remember this phrase from the Crosby Stills and Nash song?

"If you can't be with the one you love... love the one you're with."

Again, using a core BRAIN GLUE technique, they created a phrase that resonated in the minds of millions, even if they weren't fans of the group.

Okay, how about this...

Have you ever noticed how many top brands use the repeating sound of 'alliteration' in their product names?

PayPal – Coca-Cola – Bed, Bath and Beyond – Best Buy – Tik-Tok.

Do you think it's a coincidence that so many successful brands use alliteration?

How about the term *'Baby Boomers?'* Or rapper Snoop Dogg's *"Fo shizzle my nizzle,"* a slang way of saying, *"for sure, my friend."*

Does alliteration make these phrases "stick in your brain like glue?"

The answer? *"Fo shizzle my nizzle..."* meaning, yes, exactly.

Yes, You Can Apply This To A Surprisingly Wide Range Of Situations

I recently saw an ad for J-B Weld, with the slogan, *"The World's Strongest Bond."* Do you think their sales are greater than those of Gorilla Glue?

Probably not. Even if J-B Weld's bond is stronger, Gorilla Glue's name sticks in the brain like glue... pun intended.

How about this.

A friend selling material for construction sites with a product called 'Slope Block,' was telling me how he struggled for years, trying to turn his incredible product into a success.

It's only when he came up with a better way to describe it, with the slogan, *"Better Than a Retaining Wall,"* and focusing on the erosion protection properties of his product for homeowners and industrial property owners, that his revenues skyrocketed to millions in sales.

These are all examples of how many ways BRAIN GLUE can help you get the results you want from your products, sales pitches and more.

After all...

If this can help you persuade a jury, there's almost nothing you can't do with the power of right-brain selling behind you.

How crazy is it that behavioral tools like the ones you're about to learn here could help you with so much! But it does. In fact, it works so well, you may be scratching your head at why you didn't think of this before.

What Got Me Started With BRAIN GLUE In The First Place

For me, this idea of 'sticky' ideas didn't come from nowhere.

Long before I helped found one of Southern California's leading behavioral management firms, I ran a small advertising agency in Montreal. Many of our clients were a Who's Who of American Business. And life was great.

But two things happened that changed everything for me, and helped me realize there's a whole world of persuasion that I had no clue about, and it terrified me.

First, my brother John, a sales genius, floored me with something he said to the advertising buyer at Avon Cosmetics of Canada.

As we sat in his office, the buyer told my brother,

"John, it's between you and this other company. I'd love to give you guys the contract, but frankly, your price is higher than the other guy's."

After a brief pause, my brother leaned across the buyer's desk and whispered,

"Why do you think the other guy's price is so low?"

For what seemed like an eternity, no one spoke as we all sat there in nervous silence. Then, like straight out of some textbook, the buyer responded,

"I see what you mean. Okay, here, let me get you a purchase order."

I thought my brain was going to explode. What the heck just happened??? We didn't have to lower our price or change anything. The buyer hired us BECAUSE our price was higher! Wow!

This was the beginning of my realization that selling was more than just throwing logic at buyers. There was something deeper that I didn't understand about selling and human nature, and it worried me.

Then, a few months later, I saw something that gave me a panic attack.

We had an opportunity to win the anti-drug campaign in the U.S., with what we thought was a terrific set of ads. Our ads focused on logical reasons why someone should avoid using drugs.

Then I saw the winning campaign.

As the actor cracked an egg into a sizzling frying pan, he said the fateful words,

"Okay, one last time. This is your brain. This is your brain on drugs. Any questions?"

As I watched this brilliant ad, I became almost nauseous. These simple words, combined with the exaggerated sizzling sound, triggered a powerful emotional reaction in ways I could not understand.

Before that moment, I thought we were pretty good at creating effective ads. But once I saw that ad, I realized I knew nothing about 'emotional' selling.

And it terrified me.

Between this ad and my brother's choice of words with the buyer from Avon, I became overwhelmed with self-doubt. How could I ever be effective in advertising, marketing, social media, or face-to-face selling if I didn't understand how to trigger a buyer's deepest emotions – as these advertisers could, or even like my own brother could?

But once I got over my initial panic, my scientific mind became fascinated by the idea of deep-brain selling, where we trigger the emotional centers of the brain, the exact place where decisions are made.

Over more than three decades of passionately studying this incredible subject and getting to apply it with hundreds of clients and thousands of students, I've become an advocate for the power of right-brain selling and how seemingly simple changes can turn ordinary products and pitches into extraordinary income generators... how a simple shift in what we say or how we say it could turn a feeble argument into a massively persuasive pitch.

I believe that once you learn even a small part of how BRAIN GLUE works, you will be astonished at how effortless success can be with the marketing and selling efforts you make in your life.

Finally, Here's A Formula For Creating Your Own BRAIN GLUE Power Phrases and Product Names

In my classes, I've been regularly asked if there could be a formula for creating these emotion-triggering phrases. Something virtually anyone could use to help activate the right side of your prospect's brain, so they are more likely to buy your products and ideas.

The answer, of course, is yes, and that's what I will be presenting to you in the pages that follow.

Once you begin to understand how powerful BRAIN GLUE can be in helping you get what you want at work and in your personal life, I believe the way you communicate with just about anyone, from friends and family members to co-workers, bosses, clients, and the masses, will change forever.

As you learn these secrets of emotional engagement, hopefully, your own ability to influence, persuade and sell will be greatly magnified in ways that enrich your life and the lives of those who are most important to you.

The Mechanics Of BRAIN GLUE And The Structure Of This Book

BRAIN GLUE simplifies your ability to sell and persuade just about anyone by amplifying your message so it "sticks in your listener's brain like glue."

BRAIN GLUE makes your listener DESIRE and then REMEMBER what you are selling by triggering the brain's emotion centers, where decision-making happens. So, even if they don't immediately say yes, it implants your message into their memory, so it's remembered when they are finally ready to buy or take action.

Because persuasion is one of the most essential skills you will ever use, learning and understanding how BRAIN GLUE works could be one of the most valuable skills you ever develop.

To simplify your ability to use the right-brain tools and strategies of BRAIN GLUE, the rest of this book revolves around fourteen tools with the acronym STEAM ATTRACTORS, which stands for...

- <u>S</u>etting the Right Expectation
- <u>T</u>ribal Alignment
- <u>E</u>asing Their Understanding
- <u>A</u>nalogies and <u>M</u>etaphors
- <u>A</u>nchoring to Something They Already Know
- <u>T</u>oning Your Voice So It's More Persuasive
- <u>T</u>riggering Oxytocin Chemicals in their Brain
- <u>R</u>hyming Your Way to Persuasion

- Alliteration as a Persuasion Power-Tool
- Chiasmus - an Unexpected Persuasion Tool
- Trigger-Words to Use and Avoid
- Odd and Unexpected Mental Surprises
- Rejection as a Way to Attract, and
- Sense Elevating that Heightens Mental Engagement

In the first three chapters, I'll show you how to set the stage for effective persuasion.

Then, we'll deep-dive into the specific BRAIN GLUE strategies and techniques that have delivered the most outstanding results.

Welcome to the incredible power of BRAIN GLUE!

Chapter One

Setting Expectation

Guess What's Coming

The movie Jaws begins with an attractive young woman swimming by herself in the ocean in the darkness of night. Then, she stops, quivers, and screams as she is pulled down under the water by something unseen.

In Canada, the bestselling cough medicine by far is Buckley's, where they use the fact that it tastes awful as THE reason you should trust that it works so well. Can you imagine a cough medicine that tastes so bad, they advertise it with the tagline, *"It tastes awful. And it works!"*

Both these examples illustrate the power of establishing an expectation upfront that affects your audience's perception from that moment forward.

So, what's the expectation you want your audience or prospect to have right from the start?

As author Malcolm Gladwell highlights in his book, *'Blink,'* people come to conclusions about you within a millisecond of meeting you or reading your ad, post, or email.

As they say, you never get a second chance to make a first impression. That's why book covers are so important to publishing.

The danger of not establishing the right expectation right at the start is that your audience will often get the wrong impression about you or your product. From that moment forward, it will be almost impossible to change their perception.

The remedy for this, of course, is establishing the expectation YOU want right from the start.

Tell them upfront what to expect, and they'll often see exactly what you tell them to see... or taste, in the case of Buckley's.

This Is Gonna Be Great!

In the early 20th century, when P.T. Barnum launched the Ringling Brothers Barnum & Bailey Circus, he always promoted it as *"The greatest show on earth."* Do you think having that tagline set a positive expectation and made his circus more attractive to audiences?

Michael Jackson was known as *'the king of pop.'* Many people don't realize that it was Michael himself who came up with that tagline. Do you think having everyone introduce him as *'the king of pop'* helped sell Michael Jackson?

Famed boxer Muhammad Ali used to tell everyone, *"I am the greatest!"* It was a way to intimidate his opponents. But surprisingly, as he later explained it, the person who was most affected by that moniker was Ali himself. He realized, if he was going to tell everyone that he was the greatest, he'd better live up to that. And he did. To this day, he's still considered by many to be the greatest boxer ever.

In the movie Superman II, just before a major battle scene, a minor character in the film screamed out, *"This is going to be great!"* Do you think that helped the audience brace for an exciting scene? Or even better, do you think hearing that made the scene even more exciting to audiences?

Say Something Unexpectedly True At The Start And Watch What Happens

I often have clients recognize how telling a surprisingly honest truth right from the start is a great way to help build trust and confidence in your audience.

I remember giving blood and hearing the words,

"This is going to pinch just for a moment, but it'll be over quickly."

There's a level of trust and comfort that comes from being told what's going to happen, even if it's alarming you of something unpleasant.

A financial services company I was consulting with trained their sales reps to contact a schoolmate from their childhood, an old neighbor, or someone else from their past, to try and sell them financial services. As I watched them, I realized how phony the reps felt making these calls.

A typical call started with,

"Do you remember me? What are you doing these days? Do you have kids... bla bla bla."

The conversation would go on for a while until the rep pivoted to the real reason for the call, saying they had something they thought might be interesting for the person on the other end of the phone. The typical response was, *"send me something,"* or, *"I'm not interested,"* and the financial rep would hang up feeling crappy.

This was crazy. Yet, it's standard practice for many financial services firms across America.

But...

What if we could change the call completely to deliver a totally different kind of result? After all, just about everyone quickly realizes the rep is calling to try and sell them something.

Instead, why not tell the prospect right up front,

"I'm calling because I want to sell you something.

But first, I'd like to find out how you're doing. Is that okay?"

As crazy as this sounds, it delivered better results than the reps I worked with ever expected.

Once they started telling their prospect up-front why they were calling, not only did the rep feel better – that they were being honest right from the start – but the people they were talking to were more responsive.

I'll get back to this later. But for now, realize that the more honest you can be right from the start, even if it might feel too honest at times, the more significantly an outcome could be improved.

I recently saw journalist Dan Rather interviewing actor Edward Norton. In an attempt to get the actor to open up about his frailties, he started with something like this,

"Once I recognized that I was becoming a star, my ego got really big. I don't want to get too personal, but did anything like that happen to you, once you realized you were becoming famous?"

By introducing his frailty first, he made it easier for his subject to open up about his own frailties.

In media and audience interviews I did for 'The Father-Daughter Project,' which I founded, I often began with the honest explanation that,

"For 13 years, I ran a behavioral management firm working with some of the largest organizations in the world. Then I discovered that my own relationship with my middle daughter wasn't as great as I thought. I'm supposed to be this expert in human behavior, and here I discovered that I screwed up one of the most important relationships in my own life."

There's a level of trust that comes from starting out admitting a fault or frailty you might have. Especially in a selling situation, endearing yourself to your prospect or audience right from the start by admitting a shortcoming will often help them feel more comfortable about you and what you are proposing.

However, you do it, setting an expectation with your audience can boost the likelihood that you'll get the response you want.

To do that, even before you enter an interaction with someone, be clear on what you want your prospect to believe or trust about you. Then, tell them what they can expect from the presentation they are about to go through.

In this way, you will often have a greater chance of getting the results you want from your ads, emails, social posts, and face-to-face encounters.

Chapter Two

Tribal Alignment

Really, I'm One Of You

The founders of Carbonite – a company offering Internet-based cloud storage and backup of all the information on your computers – were devoted Liberals who decided to advertise on the radio show of Rush Limbaugh, a staunch Conservative.

They recognized if they could get him to pitch their product to his audience of more than twenty-million fans, it could skyrocket sales for their fledgling company.

And it did.

If more than a million people quickly signed up for their $55-a-year service, that's more than fifty-five million dollars in revenues. Incredible!

Eventually, they pulled their ads from his show because they disagreed with his stand on a controversial topic. Instead, they went to a more suitable alternative... with shock-jock Howard Stern's radio show.

In case you missed the sarcasm in the previous statement, for those who know Howard Stern, you understand that he's probably not the best role model for Liberals or Conservatives.

But here's something that relates to both radio shows.

Like Limbaugh, Howard Stern's listeners weren't just fans. They were members of a unique 'tribe,' just as we are all members of specific tribes that help define our own self-identity.

Examples include:

- the political party we affiliate with,
- the schools we went to,
- the city or country we were born in,
- the fraternity or sorority we belong to,
- our religion or lack of religious affiliation,
- whether we served in the military and, if so, which branch we served in.

Each of these is like an exclusive club or tribe that helps define us profoundly.

Go against someone's tribe, and they will likely become almost impossible to persuade of anything.

Of course, not all tribal members are resistant to people who are not members. There's terrific college pride and competitiveness between people who went to UCLA versus USC here in Southern California. Students from each school associate more closely with fellow alums but could still do business or listen to ideas from those who attended an opposing school.

Still, there are some areas where the tribe you belong to or don't belong to could affect your ability to persuade someone successfully.

Aligning With The Right Tribe Can Make Human Connection Easier

My son was retiring from the navy to start a business. When I introduced him to a choice of successful mentors at the U.S. Small Business Administration, the one person who had also served in the navy was his obvious first choice.

In my own effort to establish a relationship with the CEO of a Fortune 100-related company, I first went to his LinkedIn page and found plenty of facts about what school he had attended, his job history, etc.

But then I discovered his Facebook page, and that opened the door to a deeper level of understanding about him. I learned that his daughter had recently gotten married, that he was an avid skier, and that he was a practicing Mormon.

In my initial discussion with him, I got to talk about 'The Father-Daughter Project,' which I had founded. Knowing he was the father of a daughter connected him to me almost instantly.

Then, I asked him about his Mormon faith. He proudly explained that Stephen Covey, author of *'The Seven Habits of Highly Effective People,'* and Willard Marriot, founder of the hotel chain, were also successful Mormons. Showing interest in his 'tribes' made it much easier for me to gain his trust and ultimately do business with him.

The point here is simple.

Identifying the 'tribes' your ideal audience is in could significantly improve your ability to get them to your side of an argument. But be careful. Taking sides could sometimes hurt more than it helps.

Anita Roddick, founder of The Body Shop, a chain of environmentally friendly cosmetics, skincare, and perfume stores, reinforced her company's reputation by becoming an advocate for environmental causes. Emblazoning her trucks and store windows with *'Save the Rainforests'* promotions helped strengthen her relationship with the 'environmentalist' tribes she was connecting with.

By contrast, aligning yourself with a specific political party or controversial issue could be both profitable and dangerous because people tend to take their political and social affiliations very seriously.

So, are you aware of the different tribes your audience is a member of?

Understanding this could significantly help in your ability to influence, persuade, and sell them.

Chapter Three

Easing Their Understanding

Simplifying What's Complicated

Elizabeth Holmes, the founder of Theranos, the healthcare startup that ultimately was discovered to be fraudulent, was a brilliant persuader. As I will discuss later, she did things that could easily be part of a textbook on persuasion.

But one of the first things she did was create a visual explanation of what she was selling in a way that made it so easy to understand, you almost felt like a fool if you didn't believe and support her vision.

What was she selling?

With just a tiny drop of someone's blood, an incredible analysis could be achieved that would uncover a wide range of diseases and health issues, unlike anything that has ever existed before.

If she could have pulled this off, it would have changed the world, with hers becoming one of the world's most influential companies.

However, what she was offering was so far beyond capability that it turned out to be more science fiction than reality, at least in today's world.

But...

How she sold her idea was brilliant and provides us all with a vision of something we'd be crazy not to emulate with our own products and ideas.

For anyone who's familiar with the original Star Trek, one of the first things that comes to mind is Mr. Spock's Vulcan hand greeting, with his middle fingers separated to form a 'V.' Although the origin is from ancient Judaism, whenever someone sets their hand in the Vulcan hand sign, people instinctively know you are referring to Star Trek.

What Elizabeth Holmes did was somewhat similar.

She would hold a tiny glass vial containing a few drops of blood between her thumb and forefinger in a way that turned that image into her trademark. Whenever you saw her two fingers holding that tiny vial with blood, you knew exactly what she was saying, that,

"In my fingers, I am holding the future of healthcare. With this tiny vial, we will be able to tell you exactly what's wrong with you, with almost no other tests needed."

Can you understand how profoundly powerful that visual was, of her holding that tiny vial between her thumb and forefinger? When Forbes Magazine featured her on their cover, it was a no-brainer to have her holding that tiny vial.

With that simple visual, she turned a complex idea into something almost anyone could understand and remember.

Jerry Kaplan was trying to raise funds for his startup, Go-Computers. While in the waiting room of venture capital firm Kleiner Perkins, he experienced a moment of anxiety. As he watched other presenters leaving the conference room with what seemed like impressive pitches, he feared his presentation wasn't powerful enough. He needed a zinger that would help them understand the exciting value of what he was pitching.

Then it came to him.

Entering their office, with a few investors sitting around the table, he took his thin leather cover holding his notepad and flung it on the table towards the investors. *"Gentlemen,"* he said, *"That is your next computer. Thin as a notepad, it will revolutionize computing forever."*

The investors lifted the notepad and examined it as if it were a real computer. They held it up, noting the thinness. Then, one of the lead investors smiled with an understanding of what Jerry was proposing. They agreed to invest $4.5 million into his startup, all because of the power of his demonstration.

One of the world's most successful motor oil salesmen would visit major automakers with a seemingly outrageous claim.

"We have the purest motor oil you can buy. Here, let me show you."

Then, he would open a bottle and pour the motor oil into his mouth.

It's definitely not something I would do. But can you imagine how persuasive and memorable that presentation was?

Why am I telling you about Elizabeth Holmes, Jerry Kaplan, and the oil salesman?

No, I don't expect you to drink motor oil in front of your prospects. But understanding ways to make it easier for your prospects to understand what you are selling can help skyrocket your results in incredible ways.

It's a simple rule of marketing and persuasion.

The easier you make it for people to understand what you are truly offering, the easier it will be to get them to buy.

Does that make sense?

Are You Sure They 'Truly' Understand

Here's an important question I like to pose in my classes.

After you explain it to them, does your prospect truly understand what your product, service, or idea is?

When Walt Disney pitched his brother and investors on his idea for Disneyland, a theme park based on characters their animation company had created, they all refused to support him. Despite his having made them rich, they couldn't understand the value of animators getting into the theme park business, so they passed. It was only later, when he described his idea on tv, showing scale models of how it would look, that they suddenly realized how incredible his idea was.

The point here is simple. No matter how clear you think your pitch or proposal is, your prospects may have a totally different understanding of what you're offering and how it could benefit them.

In one of my classes, I picked someone from the audience to help explain how to find the right keywords on Google. The audience member had invented a construction product called *'The Stud-Finder,'* to help find beams behind the walls in a house. So, into Google, we typed the phrase, *"how to find a stud,"* ...and guess what came up? Porn sites!

Proving that even Google can misunderstand what you are talking about.

Motivational speaker Zig Ziglar explained how easily the seemingly simple phrase, *"I did not say he beat his wife,"* could be misunderstood, simply by putting emphasis on different words:

- *"I"* did not say he beat his wife... someone might have said it, but it wasn't me.
- I did not *"SAY"* he beat his wife... I might have implied it, but I never actually said it.
- I did not say *"HE"* beat his wife... I said someone beat his wife, but I didn't say it was him.
- I did not say he *"BEAT"* his wife...

...and... am I talking about *TENNIS*?

If a simple phrase like this could so easily be misinterpreted, think how many ways your own texts and email messages could be communicating a totally different message than you intended.

Has anyone ever been mad at you, and you didn't understand why? Maybe they misunderstood a text or email you sent them. Unfortunately, it's more common than most people realize.

I had a woman who asked why I scream so much. I was confused until she explained,

"Every time you send an email, you use all capital letters. That's screaming."

Wow. Her comment caught me by surprise.

Needless to say, I stopped sending emails in capital letters. But still, her comments reminded me how easily the written word could transmit a totally different idea than what we are trying to present.

Making It Easier For Your Prospect's Brain To Understand

For more than two decades, my team and I have conducted interviews with prospects from hundreds of our clients in a wide range of industries. Like so many of these clients, you might be surprised at how many of their prospects misunderstood what these clients were offering, despite their initially seeming to get it.

Clients were often flabbergasted at how often many of their prospects had a misguided understanding of what was being offered. Of course, they didn't misunderstand everything. But the one thing they did misunderstand often became the stumbling block that prevented them from saying yes.

But then, we came up with a way to simplify what they were describing, and getting their prospects to say yes became a whole lot easier.

That's why clarifying your offer to make it easier to understand could significantly improve your ability to influence, persuade, and sell.

In psychology, we call this *'cognitive simplicity.'* Meaning, the easier it is for people to understand what you are selling, the easier it is to get them to say yes.

Studies have shown that sometimes even a bad idea can be easier to sell if it's easier to understand.

Of course, making your idea or product easy to understand seems obvious, doesn't it? However, applying this is not as obvious as you may realize.

For starters, different people speak different languages. Accountants speak the language of numbers. Artists the language of concepts and images. Engineers the language of how things are made.

A financial consultant I was working with suggested to a famous musician that he spend his money on a certain type of investment. He explained its potential for a 7.5 percent return on his money.

As I watched, I could see the musician's struggle with whether he should participate. So, I interjected by explaining that John Lennon had also invested in something like this, and it was instrumental in helping his estate maintain its value even after his death. This explanation was enough for the musician to say yes.

For the financial consultant, this was a reminder that a lot of people hated math in school. So, throwing numbers at someone who hates math could work against you, no matter how incredible your offer.

Speak their language, and it could be significantly easier to sell them.

But there's more.

How often do we explain something without 'clarifying' what it really means?

Like this...

If I was trying to get you to understand how plastic bottles are polluting the earth, I could say,

"Americans discard 2.5 million plastic bottles every hour."

But what does that mean? There's no perspective here. How much is 2.5 million plastic bottles? Sounds like a lot, but I have no real perspective on what it means.

But add perspective and notice how much more powerful it becomes.

"Americans discard 2.5 million plastic bottles every hour – enough to reach the moon every three weeks."

Isn't that more persuasive than just mentioning the number of bottles discarded?

How about this?

I could try explaining how inflation in Venezuela has gone through the roof. But my statement becomes more powerful when I add context.

"Inflation is so bad in Venezuela; you'd have to work a full day just to pay for one egg."

Notice how much more effective these explanations are by adding perspective.

In their book, *'Made to Stick,'* the Heath brothers give a terrific example of how easy it is to give someone a thorough explanation of something, and yet, despite the thoroughness, it's basically useless in helping them understand what we're talking about.

If I was describing a pomelo, I could say,

"It's the largest citrus fruit, with a rind that's thick but soft and easy to peel away. Inside, it has a light yellow to coral pink flesh, with a very juicy texture to slightly dry, with a taste that ranges from seductively spicy-sweet to tangy and tart."

Okay. Do you now understand what a pomelo is?

With that detailed explanation, could you answer this simple question?

"Would a pomelo taste good with orange juice?"

It's hard to answer that question, isn't it?

Instead, what if I told you,

"A pomelo is basically a supersized grapefruit with a thick and soft rind."

Although less detailed, adding perspective by comparing it to something the prospect already knows means the explanation suddenly becomes infinitely easier to understand. Doesn't it?

Hollywood producers and directors regularly use analogies when trying to pitch their movies and tv shows to investors.

The movie *'Alien'* was initially pitched as *'Jaws in space,'* referring to Steven Spielberg's blockbuster shark movie. The tv show *'Breaking*

Bad' was pitched as *'Turning Mr. Chips into Scarface.'* They recognized the power of perspective when selling their ideas.

Perspective Power Tip – Compared To What... or Near To What

Have you ever heard of the resort town of Tulum, in Mexico?

What if I told you it's Cancun's older cousin, just two hours up the coast; a gateway to the nearby Mayan ruins; part of the international party circuit; and a jungle paradise with really great night life?

Creating perspective like this, by describing it as, *"Cancun's older cousin, just two hours up the coast,"* gives you something to compare it to. We're basically saying, if you know and love Cancun, you'll probably also love Tulum. Suddenly, it feels more recognizably comfortable, doesn't it?

Then, explaining how it's *"a gateway to the nearby Mayan ruins"* let's you know it's located right by a hugely popular tourist attraction, adding to its appeal.

Finally, describing it as *"a jungle paradise with really great night life"* provides a comparison – how it's like a jungle paradise but better, because it has amazing night life.

With a description like this, it's easy to understand how this sleepy fishing village has been transformed into a booming mecca for tourists.

As I explained earlier, my friend's 'Slope Block' business skyrocketed once he added the perspective, that it's *"better than a retaining wall"* because of how it protects a property against erosion.

In another example, on the outskirts of Columbus, Ohio, Rickenbacker International Airport's air freight traffic has exploded, in a large part because of their power slogan, *"a day's truck drive to half the U.S. population,"* helping shippers understand how valuable this strategic location could be for them.

In each of these examples, adding perspective by telling where it's near or comparing to something prospects already know goes a long way to helping skyrocket results.

So, what about your own product or idea?

Like Tulum, Slope Block and Rickenbacker airport, could comparing your own product or idea to something your prospect already knows make it easier for them to say YES to you?

As with all these examples, whenever you are trying to sell a product or idea, adding perspective by comparing it to something your prospect already knows is one way to simplify their understanding.

I'll discuss this in more detail later, in the Metaphors and Analogies chapter.

Simplifying Your Message

A martial arts equipment manufacturer I had worked with developed an incredible backpack.

It was oversized so it could hold all the gear a martial artist might need, from boxing gloves to shin and elbow pads to clothing and more. Besides a huge inner section, it had nineteen pockets and pouches, including waterproof ones to hold sweaty clothes, protected ones for a computer and iPod, and hidden ones to hide money. Plus, it came in two sizes, a full-size one and one that's slightly smaller to fit in overhead bins on a plane — a truly incredible product.

He called it *'The Travel Locker'* and created a busy-looking ad because there was so much to tell about it.

The ad also showed both sizes. He wanted to include more details about all the fantastic features, but there just wasn't enough room in the ad, which was already pretty busy.

Okay. Here's a secret about advertising and persuasion.

With so much competition trying to grab your buyer's attention, you have a fraction of a moment to make your point. That's it. Fail at this, and your ad becomes just another blur in the background of your prospect's life.

So, here's the trick.

The best ads usually focus on the ONE most important feature, then use a web page, a phone call, or other interaction to deliver all the other features and benefits.

For this backpack, the most important feature was its size. This was a monster of a backpack. So, our ad needed to focus on that single feature.

Then, I was faced with a problem.

The product was called *'The Travel Locker.'* So what the hell is a *'Travel Locker?'*

I get it. It's a portable locker. But in today's world, where we are constantly bombarded with information, going back to the concept of *'cognitive simplicity,'* anything that's complicated to understand gets ignored.

So, I knew we needed a better name.

At first, I thought of calling it *'The Monster,'* but *'The Beast'* sounded better. Then I eliminated everything in the ad except a photo of the larger backpack with the headline,

"The Beast... A backpack so big that it fits ALL your gear."

And the rest, as they say, is history.

Compared to the initial ad, this simplified version delivered incredible results.

There's an important point here.

Whenever you are pitching your product or service, whether it be through your face-to-face presentations, emails, ads, social media posts, podcasts, press releases, and more, if you want the greatest chance at success – regardless of how many amazing features it has – you need to hook your prospect with a single feature, something you know will grab them. Then, only once you have their attention, can you present other features and benefits.

Okay. Now that we understand the macro of how to use BRAIN GLUE to influence, persuade and sell, let's get into the real meat of this book – the mechanics of how BRAIN GLUE works and how you can start using it to boost the persuasive power of your pitches, ads, and marketing.

Chapter Four

Analogy and Metaphor

It's Just like That, Only Different

John Gray was telling me how his book, *'Men and Women in Relationships,'* was going nowhere. Sure, it sold a few thousand copies. But with so many relationship books on the market, why should anyone buy his?

Then something strange happened.

In one of the seminars he was doing to promote the book, he said something, and all the women in the audience laughed while the men sat confused. What did the women find so funny?

A discussion about the differences between men and women ensued when one of the women, half-joking, asked, *"What planet are men from anyways?"*

His response, *"I guess men are from Mars,"* elicited more laughter from the audience.

After the event, John reflected on how this half-joke had caused such a heightened reaction in the audience. *"If men are from Mars,"* he thought, *"where are women from? I guess women are from Venus because Venus is the God of love."*

As he considered this, since the book was going nowhere, why not change the title and adapt the content to this interesting metaphor?

And the rest, as they say, is history.

John Gray's book, *'Men Are From Mars, Women Are From Venus,'* exploded off the shelves and ultimately sold more than ten million copies, making it the most successful relationship book of all time.

But what really changed to transform this modest seller into a game-changer? Could simply altering the book's title and adding a few tweaks to bring the content in line with the title be all that was necessary to turn a modest seller into a game-changer?

Absolutely, and that's what I want to cover here.

In this chapter, I'll explore the concept of applying metaphors and analogies to the name and description of your products and ideas to transform them into game-changers for you as well.

Let's start by defining what a metaphor and analogy are and how they're different.

Metaphors – The Electric Shock That Heightens Emotions

A metaphor is a word or phrase that boosts the vividness of something by comparing it to something else without using the words *'like,'* or *'as.'*

For example, referring to life as a *'rat race'* or naming a tv show *'Shark Tank,'* when we know it's not really a tank filled with sharks. It's simply a group of investors, but their fierceness can sometimes feel like you're in a tank full of sharks. Calling the show 'Shark Tank' adds a heightened sense of emotion that sticks to our brains like glue.

Rather than saying, *"the woman shouted a warning to her child,"* we can boost the emotional connection to the message by replacing the word *'shouted'* with *'barked,'* as in,

"the woman barked a warning at her child."

This adds a heightened vividness that makes the phrase more emotionally engaging.

A phrase like, *"it's raining cats and dogs,"* is more vivid and memorable than simply saying it's raining heavily.

Saying, *"no man is an island,"* is more vivid and engaging than simply stating how we need to work together to get the job done right.

If you wanted to describe someone's computer as outdated, you could search for something else that's old, like a Model T, a caveman, or moldy cheese. How about relating this guy's computer to a dinosaur with the phrase, *"his computer was a dinosaur!"*

See how using a metaphor heightens the emotional engagement of what you say or write.

There's a psychological reason why metaphors are so effective at heightening the emotional engagement of the listener or reader. Where words are left-brain triggers, metaphors activate the brain's visual, smell, and other sense parts. They require more effort because the brain suddenly has to jump from the left to the right side to paint a picture of what is being described. This attaches the image, smell, or other senses to the words you are using.

If I wanted to say, *"He's an idiot,"* I could heighten the emotional engagement by calling him a *'bird brain,'* or going further by calling him, *'a chicken-brain,'* or saying he's *'thick as a brick,'* or *'not the sharpest knife in the drawer.'*

In naming a movie about a serial killer who snuck up on his victims and ate them, *'Silence of the Lambs'* – referring to helpless lambs that sit there vulnerably as the wolf sneaks up on the herd and kills an unsuspecting victim – adds a level of brilliance that helped transform a horror film into an iconic classic, as it can for your own product, book, movie title, or idea you are trying to sell.

In the previous chapter, I told you how the extra-large backpack, initially named *'The Travel Locker,'* which already is a metaphor as it's a backpack, not a locker, was renamed *'The Beast,'* another metaphor, as it's still a backpack, not a beast. Applying this metaphor instantly turned it into a bestseller by painting a more vivid brain picture of what the product was really like.

Metaphors can provide valuable product names, where naming a detergent *Tide* makes you think of an ocean wave; naming a soap *Dove* reminds you of its mildness; naming a website *Alibaba* makes you think of the poor woodcutter who won extraordinary wealth for himself with the words, *"Open Sesame."*

Naming his product, *'Gorilla Glue,'* enabled Mark Singer to create an instantly memorable image while communicating that this glue was strong as a gorilla.

Naming his company, the *'Naked Juice Company'* helped Jimmy Rosenberg reinforce the naturalness of his product while creating a name that instantly grabs your attention. In 2005, newly created packaging that highlighted the juice's unusual name helped his company surpass industry leader Odwalla, a company owned by beverage giant Coca-Cola – highlighting the incredible power of an emotion-eliciting name in helping a somewhat small company become massively successful.

Using A Metaphor To Tell The World Your Products Are Pure Art

Swedish designer Alexander Stutterheim recently founded a clothing company featuring all-natural rainwear that is highly functional yet intensely friendly to the environment.

Recognizing the toxicity of weatherproofing that's commonly used to waterproof textiles, he instead created hooded raincoats using waxed cotton that are perfectly functional yet surprisingly lightweight.

In a market with brands like *The North Face* and *Snow Peak*, he needed a name for his brand that would resonate with buyers while highlighting the original nature of his clothing.

So, what could he name such a brand?

First, as someone proud of his heritage, he wanted everyone to know it's Swedish. So, the brand's name would probably be *'Swedish... something.'* But what?

Not 'Swedish Clothing.' That would be too trite and wouldn't communicate the highly ingenious nature of his designs.

When you think of the words *original, ingenious, smart, clever...* the word *'art'* comes to mind. The name, *'SwedishArt,'* doesn't work. It's not elegant and ingenious enough. But it's a starting point. When we think of art, what else comes to mind?

The name he came up with for his brand was *'Swedish Poetry,'* a metaphor that describes his products' subtle elegance and ingenuity.

Calling a clothing brand *'Swedish Poetry'* is certainly original and different. It's not a copy of someone else's name or some generic term that's easily forgotten. I'm willing to bet, if you saw products designed by *'Swedish Poetry,'* it would engage you enough to check them out, especially if they included hangtags and promotional displays explaining what the brand represented.

Especially among higher-end brands, coming up with a name that differentiates you while clarifying what you represent through a metaphor can significantly help cement your brand in the minds of the consumers you are trying to win, as it will for a brand like *'Swedish Poetry.'*

Of course, a metaphor can also be used to strengthen the way you DESCRIBE your product or idea.

Using A Metaphor To Build A Powerful Slogan

When trying to promote your product or idea, think of the most significant feature or benefit it offers and ask yourself, what does that remind you of?

At a time when just about every salt brand clumped, the slogan, *"When it rains, it pours,"* highlighted the unique, smooth-flowing nature of Morton Salt, helping turn it into America's dominant salt seller. Their slogan was integral to letting people know what made their salt different from everyone else's.

Telling people to *"Put a tiger in your tank"* helped Esso dominate among gas stations by implying their gas had something in it that gave a car more power than the alternatives.

Telling people to *'Let your fingers do the walking'* helped the Yellow Pages dominate business directories through the 20th century. Of course, fingers don't walk. But metaphorically, this slogan created a visual that imprinted in the minds of everyone who heard it.

Slogans like these can boost a product or idea in your prospect's mind by imprinting what makes it different, just as metaphors can help individuals gain notoriety.

Famed investor Warren Buffett is a huge fan of metaphors. Sharing colorful metaphors with the press has helped him become a darling of journalists and the public.

For example, his warning investors to not ask for advice from someone who has a stake in the game was amplified with the metaphor,

"Never ask a barber if you need a haircut."

His explaining how the future can be difficult to predict was amplified by saying,

"In the business world, the rearview mirror is always clearer than the windshield."

His explaining how it's hard to tell who a good leader is until they are faced with hard times was amplified by saying,

"Only when the tide goes out do you discover who's been swimming naked."

Metaphors like these don't just magnify the points. They transform simple concepts into visually memorable anchors that stick to the brain like glue.

"Only when the tide goes out do you discover who's been swimming naked?"

I love that line, don't you?

In her book, *'Letter to My Daughter,'* author Maya Angelou created the encouraging metaphor,

"Be a rainbow in someone else's cloud."

Using colorful metaphors like this has helped her words resonate with millions of her fans and can help you generate devoted fans as well.

I heard this terrific metaphor to help kids understand how hard it is to distinguish between good and bad people.

"Be careful who you trust. Salt and sugar look the same."

This is the same process advertising agency Key/Donna/Perlstein used to develop the most famous anti-drug campaign in history.

Starting with the concept that *'drugs fry your brain,'* the natural question is, what else gets fried?

How about eggs?

Why not create an ad with a sizzling frying pan, a man breaking an egg and dropping it into that sizzling pan while saying,

"This is your brain on drugs. Any questions?"

Using a visual metaphor like this to explain the concept of drug addiction helped strengthen the message in ways that a simple suggestion to not do drugs could not.

Using A Metaphor To Sell A Concept

I recently read an article in Business Week magazine talking about how attempts to halt global warming are often useless. To make the point, the author explains that, with more than 36 billion tons of carbon dioxide emissions being pumped into the atmosphere every year, eliminating just a few million tons will be too small to make any difference.

What metaphor could you use that would help make that point? How do you explain that, with all the worldwide efforts, the impact is still just like a *'fart in the wind.'*

Let's see. The point they are trying to make is that pulling such a minuscule amount will take centuries to have any impact at all.

The phrase the author came up with was,

"it's like trying to empty a lake with a teacup."

Doesn't that create a memorable visual that reinforces their point?

See how effective a great metaphor can be.

Creating your own powerful metaphors can be easier than many people think, with a little effort and creativity.

By the way, you can also use metaphors to turn someone OFF to a competitor's product or idea. This is something politicians often use to degrade the impact of their opponent, but can be used in just about any competitive situation.

Warren Buffett hated financial derivatives. So, he came up with the memorable metaphor,

'Derivatives are financial weapons of mass destruction.'

By anchoring derivatives to weapons of war, he was able to turn a simple criticism into a highly memorable image that stuck to millions of investors' brains like glue.

So, how about you?

Do you have a product or idea you are trying to sell? Can you come up with a metaphor that heightens its vividness in a way that makes it more interesting?

Analogies – They're Just Like Metaphors Except...

Like a metaphor, an analogy is used to explain a product or idea by comparing it to something else. But unlike a metaphor, analogies can use the words *'like,'* or *'as.'*

Where a metaphor would be, *"he's a wolf in sheep's clothing,"* an analogy would be, *"He's just like a wolf in sheep's clothing."* Almost the same, but with the word *like* or *as* included.

Otherwise, they are pretty similar.

Some popular analogies include:

- *"Life is like a box of chocolates; you never know what you're going to get,"* from the movie Forest Gump.
- *"Like a good neighbor, State Farm is there."*
- She was running around *"like a chicken with its head cut off."*
- There are so many opportunities, *"it's like a mosquito in a nudist colony."*
- Someone with incredible strength is *"strong as an ox."*

Do you recognize how analogies can help make pitches, presentations, and marketing more persuasive?

Using a Metaphor To Generate A Name For Your Product That Resonates With Buyers

Okay. Let's say you're starting a company with grooming products for men. Let's say your first product is an electric shaver for the removal of a man's pubic and body hair. What would you name your company and product?

For starters, you'd need something that was not offensive while making it easy for people to understand and remember exactly what your company and product do. Something that would enable you to build a powerful brand around it, where you could easily add more products, right?

In an almost hilarious way, using this product is like landscaping your lawn with a lawnmower. So why not call the company 'Manscaped' and the product 'The Lawn Mower®?'

That's exactly what Paul Tran did, turning his Manscaped company into a highly successful brand in just a few short years, helped in a large part by the clever names he chose.

Abigail Tucker wrote a book that became a New York Times bestseller, in a large part because of the name she chose for it.

"The Lion in the Living Room... How house cats tamed us and took over the world."

Combined with a photo of an innocent-looking kitten on the cover, the words, *'The Lion in the Living Room'* engages us with humor while making it clear what the book is about. With a name like that, it's easy to understand why it became a bestseller.

See how using the right metaphor can help skyrocket results?

Analogies and metaphors simplify your prospect's ability to understand by making what you are saying somewhat more tangible in their mind by engaging other parts of the brain – in a way, making it 3-dimensional to them.

Of course, coming up with a powerful name for your book, your product, or your company isn't the only way to use metaphors and analogies.

Using A Metaphor To Strengthen The Impact Of Your Ads

Let's say you had to come up with an ad for an insurance company where they wanted you to warn people of how many booby-traps are hidden inside many of the most innocent-looking policies.

The message they want you to communicate is,

"When you buy an insurance policy from most companies, you're basically 'flying blind.'"

What they mean is, hidden inside many of the policies out there are clauses that could hurt survivors in ways the client never considered, that would only be discovered after the client is gone, when their family needs it most.

What metaphor could you use to make your point?

Well, flying blind makes me think of someone blindfolded.

So, how about an ad where a blindfolded man is throwing an oversize dart at a huge dartboard that his wife and two kids are standing in front of, with a look of panic on their faces. Our headline could be,

"Choosing the wrong insurance could hurt your family in ways you never expected."

See how a metaphor can help you develop an emotionally engaging pitch or ad?

Using An Analogy To Simplify Something Complex You Are Trying To Explain

My own behavioral management firm had a unique process that helped accelerate the results at major companies. We used behavioral tools to make people comfortable tackling projects outside their comfort zone, and the results were incredible.

Many people don't realize that one of the greatest fears of people in management is saying, *"I don't know,"* or, *"I don't know how,"* when faced with an emotional obstacle. I'm guessing they worry that if they say, *"I don't know,"* too often, people will start wondering why they were hired in the first place since they seem to know so little.

However, in the most progressive organizations, the exact opposite is true.

Once you're getting someone to tackle a complex task that's outside their comfort zone, of course they don't know how to do it. It's outside their comfort zone, so they've probably never done anything like it before. That was part of the magic that enabled us to deliver dramatic results for so many organizations.

But how do you explain that to a new prospect who has never heard of a process like this before?

For me, coming up with an analogy or a metaphor was the answer we needed to telegraph a quick understanding of how our process could generate such incredible results, and so quickly.

In essence, we were like a personal trainer who shows up at your home every morning and pushes you to do more pushups than you would do on your own.

Of course, there's more to it than that, but using the *'personal trainer'* analogy could make relating to what we do easier to understand.

So, I'd have our people begin their explanation with this.

"Like a personal trainer who shows up at your home every day and pushes you to do more pushups than you'd do on your own, our people show up at your business every week and push your people to tackle things beyond what they would do on their own. Once your key people start tackling bigger goals, dramatic results are achieved, far beyond what they're doing now. Does that make sense?"

Notice how much easier the *'personal trainer'* analogy made the explanation of our process?

Using An Analogy to Sell An Unconventional New Product

Let's say you invented an alternative to golf. Something you could play on a regular golf course, that you believe could be more fun than having to lug a bag of clubs across nine holes.

Where a single club is all you need. A club with a small basket on the end, like a mini lacrosse stick, that lets you fling the golf ball over your shoulder to start, with a shape that lets you wedge out of roughs, and putt like a normal club when you get to the green.

First, you'd have to convince golf courses to let players use these clubs on their courses, and maybe even convince them to offer your clubs as rentals.

If you could do that, you'd be on your way to revolutionizing the game of golf in ways few people could imagine.

That's the challenge Alex Van Alen faced when he invented the *'FlingStick,'* introducing an alternative to conventional golf.

So, let's consider the ANALOGY strategy. What's another sport where traditionalists were forced to accept a new alternative?

How about ski hills, that were forced to accept a younger generation more interested in snowboarding than skiing?

This analogy became the driving force in Alex's pitches to golf courses, and later on the tv show Shark Tank, where he was able to win a wealthy investor, based on the joy he had of flinging a golf ball into a net, then hearing the ski hill analogy.

Because of this analogy, FlingStick is on track to take over golf the same way snowboarding transformed ski hills. That's the power the right analogy can have to simplify how you sell your own products and ideas!

So, What Analogy Or Metaphor Can Add Power To Your Own Product Or Pitch

As you've seen in this chapter, simplifying your listener's understanding of your product or idea by coming up with the right analogy or metaphor could greatly enhance the power of your pitch.

So, think about this for yourself. What's something your product or idea is like, and how could you integrate that into your presentation or ads? If you're serious about boosting the emotional engagement of your prospects, starting here could simplify your ability to get the results you want in ways you may never have imagined.

Chapter Five

Anchoring

I Am He And He Is Me

Connecting your product or idea to something your prospect already knows and values could make it easier to get them to buy it.

When the President of Ukraine delivered a speech to the U.S. Congress requesting aid in its war with Russia, he cleverly included mention of elements he knew were emotionally important to Americans – civil rights icon Dr. Martin Luther King, the bombing of Pearl Harbor, and the terrorist attacks on 9/11.

In his speech, he mentioned Dr. King's *"I have a dream"* speech, relating it to the dream Ukrainians have of realizing freedom from their own oppressors. Then he asked Congress to recall Pearl Harbor and 9/11, when the U.S. was attacked, relating it to the attacks Ukraine was now under.

His speech proved to be highly influential in a large part because of his connecting issues and values facing Ukraine with those Americans are passionate about.

In psychology and marketing, connecting a topic, product, or person to something your audience already knows is called *'anchoring,'* helping encourage something we call *'cognitive bias.'* When done right, anchoring can be an essential tool of influence and persuasion.

Establishing an anchor early will often create a *'cognitive bias'* that colors your prospect's perception from that moment forward.

Meaning, tell them what to expect, and they will often experience exactly that, from that moment forward.

Why is this important?

Because, when it comes to persuasion, it's too easy for someone to get the wrong idea of what you're trying to say unless you clarify it in terms they understand and are emotionally connected to.

Anchoring to something they already know will often grab your prospect's attention while making it easy for them to understand the perspective you are trying to project.

Here are a few examples.

Let's Start With A Long Line Of Thieves

In 1952, when Kemmons Wilson was launching his chain of hotels, he needed a name that would make people feel instantly positive about it.

At the time, the movie *'Holiday Inn,'* starring Bing Crosby and Fred Astaire, was hugely popular. So, it got him thinking. Why not use that name for his hotels? After all, using the name of a beloved movie would create an instantly positive emotional connection with his audience, wouldn't it?

That type of thinking helped turn Holiday Inn into an almost overnight success, in a large part, by using the name of something people already knew and loved.

The history of the term, *'Rolling Stone,'* and the people who used it for themselves tells a lot about how powerful the idea of reusing a well-known name or phrase can be.

Although no one is really sure who created it, the proverb, *"a rolling stone gathers no moss,"* was initially popularized in England in the 1500s. Then, more than four centuries later, blues singer Muddy Waters borrowed it for the title of his song, *'Rollin' Stone'.* In 1962, Brian Jones saw the Muddy Waters LP on his floor and decided to call his band *'The Rolling Stones,'* which went on to become one of the greatest bands of all time. Next, Bob Dylan wrote the song, *'Like a Rolling Stone,'* which became an instant hit three years later. Almost a decade after that, The Temptations popularized the song, *'Papa Was a Rolling Stone,'* again borrowing from what everyone else was borrowing from. Then, in 1967, music magazine *'Rolling Stone'* was born.

Gee... I wonder where the magazine's founders got the name *Rolling Stone* from.

So yes, borrowing the name of something positive and anchoring your product or service to that could tremendously boost its likelihood of success.

Take the world's richest man.

Acknowledging genius-inventor Nicola Tesla, who had been an under-appreciated underdog most of his life, Elon Musk's taking the name *'Tesla'* for his electric vehicle company helped endear him to a U.S. population that loves underdogs.

Similarly, when major computer manufacturers had corporate names like International Business Machines, UNIVAC, and Control Data, Steve Jobs brilliantly called his company *'Apple,'* instantly differentiating it from everything else while branding it as approachable and people-friendly. That unexpected name created an obsessively loyal generation of fans who self-identified as creatives, rebels, and misfits, something his iconic ads later explained.

When *Dunkin' Donuts'* founder Bill Rosenberg introduced a low-cost product made from the leftover dough in the center of a donut, he needed a name that would instantly resonate with the public. At the time, the movie *'Wizard of Oz'* was immensely popular. So, he borrowed the name *'Munchkins,'* which was used for the little people in the film. The instant success of his *Munchkins* product helped catapult his struggling company to a level of success that even he could not have imagined.

In 2006, Sophia Amoruso founded an online business offering a range of edgy and unique clothing and accessories for women. Borrowing the name from a popular album, she called her company *'Nasty Gal.'* In its early years, the edgy name helped propel her business to fame and wealth at almost breakneck speed.

Is it a coincidence that iRobot, the maker of robots for homes, industrial and military use, has the same name as the famous Isaac Asimov sci-fi novel written about forty years earlier?

The point here is simple.

As long as you are not infringing on someone's copyright or trademark, borrowing the name of something already known and using it for your own product, service, or idea could be an effective way to create instant popularity for whatever you are pitching.

That's exactly what U.S. President Ronald Reagan did when trying to get the public's approval for a somewhat controversial space-based missile defense system. Borrowing the name from the massively popular movie of the day, he called it *'The Star Wars Missile Defense System,'* clearing the way for universal acceptance.

Like Procter & Gamble taking the name *'Head & Shoulders'* from the well-known nursery rhyme, these examples highlight the power of finding something already loved by your audience and anchoring your product or idea to that for a level of accelerated emotional engagement that, in some cases could not otherwise be matched.

How About Bending The Name Of Something That's Already Well Known

Many women suffer through the day having to wear high-heeled shoes at work.

So, let's say you had a new type of shoe that easily rolls up into a small bag that fits inside a woman's purse, enabling her to remove her high heels at the end of a day and replace them with a more comfortable ballet-slipper-type shoe. Then, making the bag they come in stretchable, so she can slip her high heels inside that same bag and cleanly place them inside her purse. What a great idea!

What would you name a product like this?

What you need is a name that grabs attention, is memorable, and helps women instantly understand how it works?

Let's think about this. What are some of the words that come to mind?

Shoe, bag, comfy, foot, roll-up shoes... Maybe *'foot rolls?'*

Or...

How about *'Footzyrolls,'* borrowing from the familiarity of Tootsie Roll candies. What a fun name! *Footzyrolls!*

That's exactly what Sarah and Jenifer Caplan did with their unique shoe product, helping their sales skyrocket to millions in almost no time. They even got featured on HBO's Sex and the City without their having to pay a dime. Wow!

Here's the good news. This awesome name helped propel their amazing product to almost instant success and wealth.

Now the bad news.

Once they started generating millions in revenues, the Tootsie Rolls candy company sued them for copyright infringement.

I am not a lawyer, so I cannot give you legal advice. However, to many, this seemed like a frivolous lawsuit pursued by rich folks with plenty of time and money on their hands. But regardless, building the name of your product around the success of another product's name could be dangerous, so be careful.

More Examples Of Bending The Name Of Something Well Known

Still, there are plenty of ways to bend the name of something that's well known but not protected legally, like *'Rolling Stone'* and *'Head & Shoulders.'*

Here are a few more examples.

- *'Rock Paper Shotgun'* is the name of a successful online video gaming magazine taking advantage of the popular *'rock paper scissors'* game.
- Singer *'Alice Wonder'* is taking advantage of the popular book Alice in Wonderland.
- In 1966, the National Football League changed the name of its NFL Championship Game to *'The Super Bowl'* to take advantage of the *'Super Ball'* toy, an incredibly high-bouncing ball that was hugely popular at the time. The name, *'Super Bowl,'* sounded enough like *'Super Ball'* to create a positive, memorable imprint in the minds of the public.

- When Nabisco introduced their first chocolate chip cookies to the world, they twisted the name of the popular movie and shipping term, *Ship Ahoy!* and named their cookies, *'Chips Ahoy!'* giving it a memorable name that sang positively in the minds of the public.
- Referring to blood clots, the book *'The Clot Thickens... The Enduring Mystery of Heart Disease'* stands out and becomes memorable by slightly adapting the popular phrase, *"the plot thickens."*

Searching through a dictionary of proverbs and sayings could provide you with more adaptable ideas like these that could help boost the emotional power of your product names and pitches.

Anchoring Through Licensing And Awards

If you can afford to pay for the right to use a famous name, the benefits can often be significant.

Nike's paying basketball legend Michael Jordan helped turn *Air Jordans* into a billion-dollar brand. Likewise, gaining the licensing rights from such brands as Disney and Star Wars has proven lucrative for numerous manufacturers.

But let's say you don't have the money to pay an up-front licensing fee. Are there options?

Absolutely!

First, you don't always have to pay an upfront licensing fee. For example, the Salton company got the right to use boxer George Foreman's name on their grill for nothing up-front, transforming their failing product into *The George Foreman Grill,* which became one of the most successful products in history.

Unlike most licensing deals where you have to give them an up-front fee combined with a royalty on all products sold, the Salton Company won permission to George's name and endorsement by promising a much higher percentage of profits, and he agreed.

Discount wireless service Mint Mobile enlisted actor Ryan Reynolds as spokesman by making him a partner in the company.

So, there are plenty of ways to anchor your product or idea to some celebrity or well-known product, even if you don't have the money upfront.

Winning an award from an authoritative person or organization is another way to anchor your idea or product to something that could help you achieve accelerated success.

From Crest toothpaste winning approval of the American Dental Association to put its *'crest'* on their packaging to products winning the Good Housekeeping Seal of Approval, the J.D. Power Award, some industry or regional recognition, or recognition from a trusted publication, many significant opportunities are out there for anchoring that can propel your product or idea to transformative heights.

How About Anchoring Your Product Or Idea To A Passion-Generating Topic

We all know that passion sells.

So, how about this?

Could anchoring your product or idea to something that evokes high passion help you sell it to people who might otherwise reject it?

The answer is absolutely yes... sometimes.

Take genetically modified organisms, also called GMOs.

Sometimes called *'Frankenfoods,'* these genetically altered foods raise red flags with many consumers. Yet, burgers made by Impossible Foods and others have become hugely popular with the anti-meat crowd, despite being made directly from GMOs.

Defining these products as the antidote to a jeopardized planet has so overwhelmed the senses for so many people that the fear of eating GMO-based products seems to have become obscured by the greater emotional good that comes from non-beef-made products helping to save the planet.

So yes, anchoring your product or idea to something people are passionate about could make it more desirable, even if it was initially distasteful.

Here's another example.

Whenever people would discover that a *'leveraged buyout'* firm was interested in buying their company, it often instilled terror. They knew these firms would probably be sticking their company with massive debts, then laying off hundreds or thousands of employees to pay those debts off and make money.

To reduce anxiety and resistance, many of these buyout firms eventually repackaged themselves as *'Private Equity'* firms, removing the word *'leverage'* to eliminate or minimize the kind of opposition they usually faced.

Today, many of these firms have gone one step further by aligning themselves with something many people are passionate about. In a world where passions run deep for environmentalism and good governance, many of these firms have redefined themselves yet again, anchoring themselves to the environmental and good-governance movements by repackaging themselves as *'Impact Funds,'* a term that implies they are more focused on helping make the world better.

Politicians also live off this technique, often giving an incredibly positive name to an incredibly horrible bill.

As we've seen with plant-based meats, leveraged buyout firms, and bad politics, words matter. Anchoring your product or idea to something people are passionate about will often get them ignoring much of the negativity initially associated with it.

It's like, the shinier the object placed in front of someone, the more likely they are to miss or ignore the negativity attached to it.

Although this technique could be helpful in your own marketing, it could be even more valuable in protecting you against its immoral use when people are trying to get you feeling optimistic about something that may not be that positive.

Anchoring To The Word You Want To Own

Let's say you're in the gold investments business. Wouldn't it be great if every time someone heard or thought of the word *'gold,'* they thought of your business?

It's easy to do by taking the word *'gold'* and attaching something to its end, then using that as the name of your product or business.

That's exactly what the gold-investing company, *'Goldline'* did, helping them achieve quick and lasting success. After you hear or see their ads, from that point forward, whenever you hear or think of the word, *'gold,'* redintegration kicks in, and your brain completes the phrase by saying, *'Goldline.'*

California's *'Solar Mike'* did the same, anchoring the name of his business to the word, *'solar.'* With word-ending behavioral anchoring, he knew that once anyone heard his ad, from that moment forward, every time someone would hear the word, *'solar,'* their brain would complete the phrase – *'Solar Mike.'*

If I owned a home loan company, I always thought I'd probably call it something like *'Home Loan Joan,'* combining this type of anchoring with rhyme, another BRAIN GLUE technique that I'll be covering soon.

Attaching your name to the end of the word you want to own, and repeating it a few times to your prospect, is a classic example of anchoring at its most basic level.

Anchoring To Your Biggest Competitor

Finally in this chapter is the idea of anchoring your product to your biggest competitor, so every time someone hears your competitor's name, they also think of you.

In 1962, with Hertz dominating the rent-a-car market, Avis, a far distant number two, anchored itself to the Hertz name with the advertising campaign, *"We're number two... when you're only No. 2, you try harder... or else!"* and saw their revenues skyrocket. As Avis proved, highlighting your underdog status by calling yourself the alternative to an industry leader can prove highly lucrative.

In the early 1960s, Coke and Pepsi dominated the soft drink market, with more than 80% of all soft drinks being colas. A few years later, 7-Up launched *'The Uncola'* ad campaign, positioning itself as the alternative to colas, and their revenues doubled almost overnight.

In 1978, Susan Striker came up with an alternative to conventional coloring books for kids with *'The Anti-Coloring Book.'* Her innovative book had kids completing partially drawn images first, then coloring them in. Her first *'Anti-Coloring Book'* became an instant success and ultimately led to launching a successful brand, where more than a dozen versions have since been published.

For her, having a name like *'The Anti-Coloring Book'* meant that every time someone thought of a coloring book, *'The Anti-Coloring Book'* would also come to mind.

Don't Forget That Anchoring Is One Of The Great Power Tools Of Persuasion

What we've seen from these examples of *'anchoring'* is that connecting your product or idea to something already known by your audience could give it instant attention-grabbing abilities while making it almost impossible to forget.

So, for yourself, here's something to consider.

What would you want to anchor your product or idea to that instantly creates a positive impression in your prospect's mind?

Or, if it's a competitor you are trying to diminish in your prospect's mind, what could you anchor their product or idea to that triggers a negative emotion?

Applying this could significantly improve the outcome you are seeking.

Chapter Six

Toning Your Voice

A Screech by Any Other Name

Could the sound of your voice be holding you back from being more persuasive?

Margaret Thatcher was told her voice was too unemotional and too screechy to be taken seriously in British politics. It wasn't until she hired a voice coach, who lowered the timbre of her voice, slowed the speed at which she spoke and increased the emotional emphasis she had on certain words, that she was finally elected head of her political party and eventually, Prime Minister of England.

Elizabeth Holmes, the founder of the fraudulent Theranos healthcare company, was able to raise almost a half-billion dollars from investors, aided in part by the impressiveness of her artificially deep voice.

As the menacing voice of Darth Vader in the original Star Wars films, and then, as the commanding signature voice announcing, *"This... is CNN,"* actor James Earl Jones conquered a lifetime of stuttering to become one of the most authoritative voices of our time with the help of voice training.

So, what about you?

Do you find yourself fighting too hard in your attempt to be heard? Does your impatience force you to interrupt, creating a sense of urgency in your voice and demeanor? Could people hear the straining in your voice as you speak? Could that be hurting your ability to persuade in ways you don't even realize?

In the movie *'The Godfather,'* actor Marlon Brando showed us that someone with great power doesn't need to shout or strain his voice to get people to listen. The most persuasive people are listened to, even when they whisper.

I came from a family where you had to fight your way into a conversation to get heard. That forced me to raise my voice and struggle to interrupt, so I could get anyone to listen to my ideas. The strained speaking style I developed, as a result, reduced my ability to influence, persuade and sell effectively, regardless of how valuable my contribution would be.

As I became more knowledgeable and aware in the world of behavioral management, I began to realize that embracing the mantra of *'calm confidence'* would change everything for me. And it did, in almost miraculous ways.

Even without voice coaching, owning the inner feeling of *'calm confidence'* could significantly improve your ability to persuade and command authority in ways you may never have considered, as it has for me.

I'm not saying you cannot succeed with a screechy or unimpressive voice. You certainly can. However, the road to greatness and happiness could be easier when you become the embodiment of self-confidence.

Once I owned that mantra, becoming the head of a breakthrough ad agency and later founding one of America's leading behavioral management firms became significantly easier.

So, how about you?

Could owning the mantra of *'calm confidence'* help you reach your most important goals easier than you ever realized?

Maybe.

Heck, it might even help you become Prime Minister of England!

Chapter Seven

Triggering Oxytocin

How Laughers Are Buyers

Could telling a joke, even a bad one, make it easier to get someone to buy your product or idea?

In surprising ways, the answer is yes. Here's why.

Let's take two hormones that affect our mood – cortisol, and oxytocin.

Cortisol is a stress hormone that triggers the fight-or-flight response in us. It gets released into our body whenever we are mad or scared, coursing through our bloodstream and staying there for up to thirty-six hours.

This means, if someone is mad or scared at anything, they will likely be resistant to your product or idea and could stay resistant to saying yes to just about anything for more than a day.

This doesn't mean you can't get that person to buy anything. But getting them to agree to something important may be more difficult than it needs to be.

By contrast, when someone or something makes us laugh or grabs our intense fascination, our body releases the hormone oxytocin. Also called *'the love hormone,'* oxytocin is the antidote to cortisol, making relationship-building and persuasion easier. Oxytocin in our bloodstream waters down the effects of cortisol, making people more receptive to what we are proposing.

That's why joke-telling can be such a powerful negotiating tool.

One of America's top attorneys told me how his ability to get a judge and a jury to laugh will often help him win seemingly impossible cases.

U.S. Presidents Ronald Reagan and Bill Clinton recognized the power of humor and used it regularly to win over opponents and endear themselves to the public.

I remember seeing photos of Bill Clinton laughing with Russian President Boris Yeltsin and knowing right away the relationship between our two countries was safe.

President Ronald Reagan won reelection in a landslide, in a large part because of his ability to make everyone laugh. In fact, during the 1984 presidential debates, he was asked by the moderator if, at 73, he was too old to be president. He responded with,

"I will not make age an issue of this campaign. I am not going to exploit, for political purposes, my opponent's youth and inexperience."

His response was so unexpected, it caused uproarious laughter even from his opponent, Walter Mondale, instantly transforming the mood of the debate and the election.

Could Humor Be More Important Than Relevance

Although touching and hugging a loved one can also trigger oxytocin, the ability to make someone laugh has been attributed to relationship building on many surprising levels. In fact, many couples and psychologists believe the secret to a long marriage is being with someone who makes you laugh.

Besides its ability to make your prospect more receptive to your ideas, in the chapters that follow, you will also notice how constructing your argument as a joke could even take a ridiculous position and make it *'feel'* plausible.

Jokes are great examples of how, when you trigger the brain's emotional side, you may not even need logic to make your argument persuasive.

Take these two examples.

"You can't hug a child with nuclear arms,"

and,

"The right to bear arms is almost as crazy as the right to arm bears."

Although both these phrases are ridiculous from a logical standpoint, because they are phrased somewhat humorously, their persuasive power is amplified in ways a straightforward statement cannot.

Which helps us understand the power of humor when we are seriously trying to influence, persuade and sell just about anyone.

Remember this.

Ignoring this power... is not something to laugh at.

Chapter Eight

Rhyming

How A Poem Will Own 'Em

I'm surprised that few psychologists seem to mention *'redintegration,'* when this could be one of the most important elements contributing to persuasion and human interaction.

As I mentioned earlier, redintegration refers to the instinctive need we have for completion.

If I start saying something, you want to... complete it, don't you?

Redintegration is why we love symmetry, poetry, and other patterns in speech, visuals, text, ads, etc. It's why we need to answer questions, isn't it?

It's why we watch crappy tv shows to the end. Because once a problem is identified, we need to find out how it resolves.

It's why we need to experience justice. Once we recognize that someone committed an injustice, our brain and nervous system want to see that it gets punished or fixed.

It's why, when we hear a mistake, we need to speak up and correct it, like this,

"Autocorrect makes a word of difference."

In case you missed that, it should have said, *"autocorrect makes a WORLD of difference."*

Redintegration is why we like to see patterns, why we are attracted to faces that are symmetrical. It's also why non-symmetrical images and unexpected patterns and situations grab our attention.

The movie, *The Sixth Sense* – with the famous phrase, *"I see dead people"* – became a blockbuster hit because, once it was revealed at the end that the main character was actually dead too, redintegration made people need to re-watch the movie so they could observe all the clues that they missed the first time they watched the movie.

In the upcoming chapters, I'll be showing you the many patterns that attract and sell us, including rhyme, alliteration, chiasmus, trigger words, and odd combinations of words and phrases.

For now, let's start with rhyme.

Rhyme works incredibly well at helping convince people, because it has a pattern that sticks in the brain, making your rhymed phrases easier to remember and more engaging than simple statements.

But rhyme also triggers something in the emotional centers of the brain, where decisions happen, enabling a rhyme to have incredible persuasive powers.

First, let's address how rhymes are easy to remember.

I was chatting with my grandkids on a zoom call. As we were ready to end the call, I said, *"see you later, alligator,"* and prodded them to respond with, *"in a while, crocodile."*

Funny how something I learned as a kid would still be stuck in my brain decades later. Even on my death bed, I bet I'd be able to recite that rhyme and many others that I learned way back in my childhood.

Think of all the nursery rhymes you've heard as a kid.

Do any of these sound familiar?

- It's raining; it's pouring; the old man is snoring.
- Hickory Dickory Dock. The mouse ran up the clock.
- Jack and Jill went up the hill.
- Little Miss Muffet sat on her tuffet.

- Rain, rain, go away, come again another day.
- Little bo peep has lost her sheep.
- Liar liar, pants on fire.

I'm guessing these are not phrases you regularly share at work or in the grocery store. You probably haven't heard them for years or even decades. Yet, if I started one that you heard as a child, I bet you could recite it as if you heard it yesterday.

This is why rhyme can be such a powerful BRAIN GLUE tool for you. It sticks with you, even without trying.

Have you ever heard this?

"I've been standin' on a corner in Winslow, Arizona, such a fine sight to see.

It's a girl, my lord, in a flatbed Ford slowing down to take a look at me."

This iconic lyric from the song, *'Take It Easy,'* not only helped The Eagles become one of the most successful bands of all time. It also turned the tiny town of Winslow, Arizona, into a major tourist attraction, along historic Route 66.

With so many people visiting the town each year because of that song, they decided to erect a statue on that very corner, with a guy leaning on a lamp post with the engraved words, *"standin' on the corner,"* providing visitors with an engaging photo opportunity.

What's funny about this rhyming phrase's power is that it was never intended as a promotion for the town. Yet, hearing it pushed psychological buttons inside the brains of enough people that the town has celebrated an incredible tourist trade as a result.

That's the power of rhyme as a BRAIN GLUE mental engagement tool.

To Get Your Creativity Going, Here Are A Few More Ideas

Let's say you wanted to get people coming to a sale you had in your store. The phrase, *"shop til you drop,"* might help get people engaged enough to bring them right to you.

An attorney or car repair shop using the term *'fender bender'* in its ads and promotions could engage prospects better than just mentioning the word *'accident.'* Similarly, a repair shop calling itself *'The tender fender-bender mender'* could build quite an audience with a name like that.

Arguing that a certain type of writing instrument is *'too cool for school'* could be strong enough to convince millions of kids to buy your product.

Terms like *'shop til you drop,'* the *'blame game,'* and *'double trouble'* stick to the brain so well, you could probably create a board game with any of these terms, and people would want to check it out simply because of how that name engages the same parts of the brain that trigger buying emotions.

The owners of Lassus Gas Stations in the Indiana and Ohio areas decided to open *'Handy Dandy'* convenience stores, capitalizing on the power of that rhyming name to attract customers.

Have you ever had *'Famous Amos'* cookies? Wally Amos built an incredibly successful brand of cookies on the rhyming power of the name he came up with. Of course, they were delicious cookies. But there are plenty of delicious cookie brands out there that never experience even a fraction of the kind of success his did. Do you think the name *'Famous Amos'* helped? Of course, it did!

The success of the *'Squatty Potty'* toilet stool that I mentioned earlier, is a great example of how a rhyming name could give your product or brand that extra boost it needs to sell like crazy.

You could easily use terms like *'boy toy'* and *'double trouble'* to make a point because their rhymes stick so solidly in the brain.

Using Rhyme To Win A Court Case

As I covered earlier but continue to refer to because it's such a profound example, the rhyming phrase,

"If the glove don't fit, you must acquit,"

...turned Johnnie Cochran into one of the most famous attorneys on the planet because of its ability to get his client, OJ Simpson, off from an almost certain guilty verdict, despite overwhelming evidence against him.

As OJ's attorney, he knew the most incriminating piece of evidence was a glove found at the murder scene that supposedly belonged to the killer. If there was some way he could use that glove to cast doubt on his client's guilt, he knew the result could be monumental.

Let's follow his probable thinking process.

Knowing the glove was the critical piece of evidence he wanted to use, trying to come up with the right piece of persuasion, he could have started with three elements – *glove, fit,* and *acquittal.*

So, what rhymes with the word, *'acquit?'*

"If the glove don't fit, you must acquit."

He also used the word *'don't'* instead of *'doesn't'* to keep the phrase sounding street-smart and natural.

Another attorney would probably have said,

"if the glove doesn't fit, you have to release my client."

But Johnnie Cochran recognized that a poem would resonate so strongly in the jurors' minds that they would practically be forced to free his client, especially if OJ could demonstrate that the glove didn't really fit him at all, by struggling to put it on, which he did.

If rhyme works so well in a murder trial, where else could it work?

Using Rhyme To Kill A Competitor

In the early part of the twentieth century, an alarming number of people were dying from pellagra, a disease brought on by a deficiency in vitamin B3. Just about every part of our body needs it to function properly, while it also helps lower cholesterol, ease arthritis, and improve brain function. A diet absent of vitamin B3 would bring on painful, if not deadly symptoms.

During this time, Wonder Bread had become the dominant bread seller in America by introducing the first sliced bread, around 1930.

Have you ever heard the phrase, *'it's the best thing since sliced bread?'* Well, this is what they were referring to.

About a decade after its introduction and dominance, it was discovered that Wonder Bread was so deficient in vitamin B3 that it might have been one of the greatest contributors to the pellagra outbreak in America.

Seizing on this discovery, Wonder Bread's competitors came up with a phrase that spread across America like wildfire,

"The whiter your bread, the quicker you're dead."

This phrase proved so powerful in hurting Wonder Bread's sales that their income started taking a nose-dive for the first time in a decade.

To solve this, they developed a process to fortify their bread with niacin, one of the greatest sources of vitamin B3. Their solution introduced the idea of fortifying foods with vitamins and minerals, which has become common practice throughout the food industry to this day.

What's significant is, this change would never have happened without the power of that rhyming phrase,

"The whiter your bread, the quicker you're dead."

So, if you have a competitor with an inferior product that you are trying to displace, coming up with a rhyme could be the answer you're looking for.

Using Rhyme To Build Your Own Personal Brand

Motivational speaker Zig Ziglar gained a significant reputation for himself, in a large part, because of his 'Zig-isms,' often using rhyme and alliterative phrases that helped turn many of his quotes iconic.

One of his most memorable is,

"We all need a daily checkup from the neck up to avoid stinkin' thinkin' which ultimately leads to hardening of the attitudes."

Notice how this phrase relies heavily on rhyme as well as alliteration, which will be discussed in the next chapter. These brain-engaging tools helped make its point while transforming a simple suggestion into something memorable that has connected emotionally with millions of people. Slogans like this have helped Zig stay relevant and iconic even years after his death, in what had become the highly competitive motivational industry.

Dr. Seuss became an iconic children's book author with rhyming quotes like this,

"Today, you are you! That is truer than true!

There is no one alive who is you-er than you!"

I recently saw this quote,

"Twinkle twinkle little star, point me to the nearest bar."

The author is anonymous, but coming up with rhyming quotes like this is a great way to develop and strengthen your own personal brand.

By the way, this guy who's named *'anonymous'* sure has a lot of quotes.

That's a joke...

Using Rhyme To Sell A Product

In marketing, we're always looking for a differentiator that gives people a unique reason to buy from us rather than from a competitor. Once we find or develop this unique differentiator, turning it into a clever rhyme will often help skyrocket our results in ways that non-rhyming phrases rarely can.

In the 1960s, famed advertiser Claude Hopkins was hired to develop a slogan for Pepsodent toothpaste. Focusing on its ability to whiten teeth, his quest led him to the slogan,

"You'll wonder where the yellow went, when you brush your teeth with Pepsodent."

This phrase highlighted the main benefit of using Pepsodent and helped the product become a huge success. However, the company was slow in adopting fluoride to their product. Suddenly, competitors had a greater claim to the benefit of whiter, stronger teeth, forcing the company to drop its winning slogan eventually.

Today, Pepsodent is relegated to the shelves of discount stores, selling for about half the price of its competitors.

The reason for its ultimate failure should be a lesson to all of us.

Once you have a powerful slogan, that should become your mission statement. If Pepsodent made its fortune by touting its incredible tooth-whitening power, it needed to stay ahead of competitors as the best tooth-whitening product that's out there.

Today, the most profitable versions of major toothpaste brands focus on their superior tooth-whitening capability. Had Pepsodent used its winning slogan as a beacon, it could have continued to dominate a category that continues to resonate with consumers.

Going back to our Timex story, in the early 1960s, the company developed an impact-resistant waterproof watch they believed gave them a competitive edge over the more fragile timepieces that populated the watch world. They knew, if they could find a way to communicate this unique feature to the public, it would turn their watches into an absolute goldmine for them.

To develop a catchphrase that would resonate with just about everyone who heard it, they probably started by listing all the words associated with their watch and its advantage.

Words like,

watch, waterproof, impact-resistant, indestructible, striking, ticking.

They would probably have gone through a list of words that rhymed with each of these. When they got to the word *'ticking'*, which also connects with our Sense-Elevation tool that will be discussed a little later, the word *'licking'* would eventually come up.

Wow! – ticking, licking... *"It takes a licking and keeps on ticking?"*

This process might seem a little tedious until you realize the slogan they came up with was so powerful, it enabled them to dominate the watch market while generating more income and profit than they ever imagined.

Combining Sense-Elevation, which will be discussed soon, along with Rhyme helped transform Timex and the campaign that launched it into legendary status, just as it could for your own product or idea.

Using Rhyme And Pacing To Clean Up The Environment

Here's one more example of how rhyme could help you uncover an engaging catchphrase that gets people doing what you want. In this case, it's not just the rhyme itself, but also the pacing of the beats that delivered such significant results.

Pacing? Yes, pacing, meaning the number of beats or syllables in each of your sentences.

In the early 1970s, the United States Forest Service created the *'Woodsy Owl'* mascot to get young kids to help protect the environment. When you consider their primary goal, the words *"don't pollute"* immediately come to mind.

With the owl as the mascot, the obvious slogan became,

"Give a hoot – don't pollute."

This simple phrase proved to be memorable and effective, not just with kids but with everyone who heard it.

Fast-forward to today, where their current motto is,

"Lend a hand—care for the land!"

Although the slogan rhymes, its effect is diminished because each phrase has a different number of syllables.

Give a hoot... 1-2-3.

Don't pollute... 1-2-3.

Compare that to,

Lend a hand... 1-2-3.

Care for the land... 1-2-3-4.

My wife likes to remind me of the brilliance of children's book author Theodor Geisel.

Also known as Dr. Seuss, Geisel clearly understood that keeping the number of beats in his rhymes equal made them resonate more effectively in the minds of the children and adults who hear them.

In his book, *"How the Grinch Stole Christmas,"* he famously wrote,

"Maybe Christmas," he thought, "doesn't come from a store.

Maybe Christmas...perhaps...means a little bit more!"

Each phrase has the same number of beats, making his words dance in our brains with joy and resonance.

Remember, the brain likes simplicity.

This means, if you want a rhyming phrase with the greatest impact, you may consider not only having your phrases rhyme, but also having them contain the same number of beats.

Applying Rhyme And Pacing To Your Own Products And Ideas

Throughout this chapter, I've discussed the power of rhyme in helping you develop a memorable and motivating name or slogan for your product or idea. We've discovered that it wasn't just marketers. That even a world-famous attorney used rhyme to get his client freed.

Like the rest of the tools in this book, rhyme sticks your idea to your prospect's brain like glue. When done properly, people will remember a rhyming phrase, years and even decades later.

This is why you need to connect the phrase you come up with to the most significant benefit or differentiator of your product or idea.

I recently saw an ad for the Korean car brand, Kia, using the slogan,

"We wanna see ya in a Kia."

Is that phrase memorable? Yes.

But does it give you a reason to buy the car? No.

Compare that to the phrase, *"It took a licking and kept on ticking,"* or even the name, *"Squatty Potty,"* and you begin to understand how the right name or slogan can propel you to heights unimaginable even to your greatest fans.

And it can keep you there if you make sure it delivers the message you want.

So, before you leave this chapter, ask yourself these questions.

- Why is your product or idea important?
- What makes it different?
- What are some keywords that describe your product or its features?
- How can you create a rhyme that defines what's unique about your product or idea?

Like the nursery rhymes we heard as kids, your audience will remember your phrase forever if you can do this right. But, unlike those nursery rhymes, it will also deliver the decisions you are seeking for your product or idea.

Chapter Nine

Alliteration

Using Silly Sounding Syllables To Sell

What do *"Peter Piper picked a peck of pickled peppers"* and, *'Coca-Cola,'* have in common?

Both are examples of alliteration, the repetition of sounds.

Until I started exploring this, I never realized how often alliteration is used to develop robust product names, phrases, and brands.

Let's start with product and business names.

How about...

Best Buy, PayPal, Tik Tok, Dunkin' Donuts, Roto-Rooter, Jelly Belly, Burt's Bees, Captain Crunch, Jungle Jim, Lululemon, Muscle Milk, KitKat, M&Ms, Ted Talks, Bed Bath and Beyond, Chocolate Chip Cookies, Rocky Road Ice Cream, Meals on Wheels, Pooper Scooper, Silly Putty, Hula Hoop, YoYo.

How about movie names?

Beauty and the Beast, Pink Panther, King Kong, Peter Pan, Doctor Dolittle.

How about the names of famous celebrities?

Chevy Chase, Marilyn Monroe, Marilyn Manson, Jesse Jackson, Michael Moore, Ronald Reagan, Barack Obama, George Jetson,

Killer Kowalski, Kit Carson, Joan Jet, Little Leroy... Okay, the last one I made up. But I think you get the idea.

How about famous terms like these?

Cape Cod, Baby Boomers, Bed Bugs, Cash Cow, Hip-Hop, March Madness, Terrible Twos.

How about famous expressions?

Cool as a Cucumber, Cream of the Crop, Dead as a Doornail, Easy Peasy, Live and Let Live, Super-Size, Sink or Swim, The More the Merrier, Trash Talk, Trick or Treat, Set It and Forget It.

Is it a coincidence that each of these uses the repeating sound of alliteration?

Absolutely not.

Names and phrases that use alliteration tend to stick solidly to our brain's memory and decision centers.

Whenever our brain hears a repeating sound, it groups the sounds together through parts of the brain that process images and sounds. This is the same part that engages emotions. That's why an alliterative phrase can be so attention-getting and memorable.

Motivator Zig Ziglar punched up the power of his quote,

"Attitude, not aptitude, determines altitude,"

...making it memorable and more meaningful, as did author Eugene Bell Jr with his quote,

"Aspire to inspire before we expire."

Although alliteration clearly elevates the power of quotes like these, using it to name products is even more common.

Think about it.

Doesn't the name *'Airbnb'* grab your attention more than *'Expedia'* and *'Bookings.com?'*

Doesn't the name *'TikTok'* grab your attention more than *'Facebook?'*

You may not realize it, but it does, because the brain processes it with mental connections that are not present with most common words and phrases.

On a publishing site that I was scanning, I saw a book called *'The Big Bad Book of Botany.'* I instantly thought it might be something worth checking out. Then, I realized I had enough to read and passed. But because it had an alliterative name, it grabbed my attention enough to get me reading its description.

Could A Simple Change Cause A World Of Difference

In Quincy, Massachusetts, Bill Rosenberg's business was struggling despite having incredible products.

For starters, to attract a large, dedicated audience to his Open Kettle doughnut shop, he introduced fifty-two incredible doughnut flavors. Then, to counter the horrible-tasting, often mold-tainted coffees sold by most local coffee shops, he offered the same premium coffee as some of the best hotels in the city.

Still, people were not flocking to his shop.

Then he got an idea. Could the name of his shop be part of the problem? What if he had a better name than Open Kettle? Could that make a difference?

Since he was selling doughnuts, he realized the word doughnuts should probably be in the name. But what else could he add that would make his shop's name distinctive? He asked an employee how people used the donuts, and the response... *"They dunk it in the coffee."*

Aha! Let's call it *'Dunkin' Donuts'* and see what happens. Even the sound of those words together, *'Dunkin' Donuts'* sounds appealing, doesn't it?

Changing the sign out front suddenly caused an avalanche of customers, transforming his struggling business into a massive success. Proving that yes, the name of your product or business could make a huge difference.

That's the power of alliteration.

Procter & Gamble doubled sales of their shampoos by adding three simple words to their labels: *'Rinse and Repeat.'* Regardless of how subtle you might think this is, the effectiveness is amplified with alliteration.

Amazon's Chinese competitor, *'Alibaba,'* even with its stock symbol BABA, has grown to become a mega-brand incredibly fast with the help of a name that twinkles with alliteration.

Board games like *'Hungry Hungry Hippo'* and *'Chinese Checkers'* have thrived in a large part because of their alliterative titles.

Let's say you wanted to create a slogan for your super-absorbent paper towel brand. Could alliteration maximize its memorability?

How about calling it Bounty, *'the quicker picker-upper?'* Wouldn't that make, not just the name of the product but the main benefit it delivers more memorable, especially when you're in the store ready to buy?

Cable tv's news satire show, *'Full Frontal,'* starring Samantha Bee, benefits from an alliterative name, as does *'Shake Shack'* restaurants.

How about this.

To give singer Stefani Germanotta a more memorable stage name, her first record producer came up with the name, *'Lady Gaga,'* stealing it from rock group Queen's song, Radio Ga Ga... With the help of her antics as a performer and her talent as a singer-songwriter, Lady Gaga has dominated music and films in a large part because of her unforgettable name.

What About Yours

Before my research into the power of BRAIN GLUE, I never realized how many amazing brands, ideas, and people had been boosted because of alliteration. Did you?

Using alliteration to enhance the influence and memorability of products is a secret of top branding companies, that almost no one will share with you... until now. With a bit of creativity, it can become a valuable tool to help boost the power of your own products and ideas.

So, where do you start?

Here are a few questions that will help...

- Do you have a product or idea you are trying to get people to buy?
- What is the main benefit it offers to your prospect?
- What are some of the words you can use that describe this benefit?
- What are some of the words that use the same sounds?

Answering these questions could help get your juices flowing towards a name or description that amplifies what you are selling in a way that simplifies your ability to get people to say yes.

Chapter Ten

Chiasmus

When Opposition Attracts

I'm old enough to remember President John F. Kennedy saying these historic words in one of his famous speeches...

"Ask not what your country can do for you. Ask what you can do for your country!"

I didn't realize how he was using a technique called chiasmus to turn a simple phrase into an iconic benchmark of American history.

As we now understand, our brains like patterns. It's why poetry "sticks to the brain like glue." It's also why chiasmus sticks.

Here's how chiasmus works.

Chiasmus takes a two-part phrase or sentence and reverses the meaning or structure of the second part. A prime example is...

"A man who stands for nothing – will fall for anything."

See how *'stand for nothing'* and *'fall for anything'* are opposites.

Like rhyme and alliteration, chiasmus triggers different parts of the brain, making phrases that use it more engaging and memorable.

Technically, even though it's chiasmus-like, when the WORDS in both parts of a phrase are repeated, it's called *'antimetabole.'*

Here are a few examples.

"Winners never quit, and quitters never win."

Notice how the words *'win'* and *'quit'* are repeated?

"When the going gets tough, the tough get going."

"Eat to live, don't live to eat."

These are *'antimetabole'* examples, whereas, when an opposite concept is presented, that's called *'chiasmus,'* as with these...

He knowingly *led*, and we blindly *followed*.

When nothing goes *right*, go *left*.

Remember to *forget*.

In essence, *antimetabole* and *chiasmus* are basically the same. So, for simplicity's sake, regardless of whether the words repeat or not, I will refer to everything in this chapter as *'chiasmus.'*

Chiasmus can add incredible power to the talks you give, the ads you create, and even the comedy you write.

Early film star Mae West shocked and delighted audiences by her use of chiasmus, with lines like these...

"It's not the men in your life that matters; it's the life in your men."

"It is better to be looked over than overlooked."

"Women like a man with a past, but they prefer a man with a present."

"When women go wrong, men go right... after them."

"Good girls go to heaven; bad girls go everywhere."

And reversing the popular saying, *"A good man is hard to find,"* she created the suggestive,

"A hard man is good to find."

Mae West's popularity was built on her bawdy persona, which was expressed in a large part through quotes like these.

Someone who also understood the power of chiasmus was civil rights activist Malcolm X. To amplify his point that Blacks were brought to America against their will, he coined the iconic phrase,

"We didn't land on Plymouth Rock; the rock landed on us."

Notice how much more power his idea has once chiasmus is applied?

Top advertisers reveled in the power of chiasmus with slogans like these...

"I'm stuck on Band-Aid, 'cause Band-Aid's stuck on me,"

"Starkist doesn't want tuna with good taste; Starkist wants tuna that tastes good!" and

"Shaefer is the one beer to have when you're having more than one."

Whenever you are trying to sell an important concept that you want to "stick in their brain," present it with chiasmus, and it can become infinitely more impressive.

Euripides, the playwright from ancient Greece, is often remembered for famous lines like this that are still referenced more than two thousand years after his death...

"I'd rather die on my feet than live on my knees."

As I mentioned previously, although I personally am not opposed to the right to bear arms, I was impressed with the persuasive power of this phrase by British comedian Chris Addison.

"The right to bear arms is slightly less ridiculous than the right to arm bears."

As ridiculous as this phrase's logic is, its persuasive power is magnified by how chiasmus stimulates the brain's emotion centers, where decisions are formed.

Meaning, you may not even need logic to persuade someone. If there's a way to trigger the brain's emotional pathways, you may be able to persuade in ways that logic could never achieve.

To me, that's pretty frightening, knowing that logic may be less important if you can push behavioral triggers in your prospect's brain. The good news is, in most cases, the mind doesn't really work that way. Rarely will emotional triggers be all that's needed to sway someone to your way of thinking.

However, even with powerful logic, you will often still need emotional engagement to get your prospect to cross the finish line, which is why chiasmus and the other tools in this book can be so important.

How about this.

I know people who like to avoid conflict. It can be a good thing, but there are times when avoiding conflict can work against you.

So, let's say I wanted to help someone understand that avoiding conflict may not always be the best idea. Applying the chiasmus model, the idea of avoiding conflict is like trying to keep the peace, isn't it? The opposite of peace is *war*. So, how about putting the words *peace* and *war* together in a sentence to highlight the point.

Author Cheryl Richardson did exactly that with the phrase,

"If you avoid conflict to keep the peace, you start a war inside yourself."

On another front, Zig Ziglar was frustrated that so many people who attended his seminars never actually applied what he was teaching. So, long before Nike developed the *"just do it"* slogan, Zig coined the chiasmus phrase,

"You don't have to be great to start, but you have to start to be great."

Doesn't that resonate more than simply asking someone to try it?

Here are a few more examples of the engaging power of chiasmus.

Recording mogul Russell Simmons coined the phrase,

"Needing nothing attracts everything,"

Fitness entrepreneur George DiGianni introduced the idea,

"Being told the truth is rarely as hurtful as discovering a lie."

Designer John Bielenberg came up with the phrase,

"In design, thinking wrong is right."

See how this works?

Benjamin Franklin highlighted the importance of planning properly with the phrase,

"Failing to prepare is preparing to fail."

Seventeenth-century politician Anthony Weldon introduced the phrase,

"Fool me once, shame on you; fool me twice, shame on me."

Isn't it amazing how a phrase like that, built on chiasmus, has remained relevant and remembered even centuries after it was first coined?

Investor Warren Buffett loved using chiasmus. When sharing the investment strategy that helped him become the world's richest man, Buffett explained,

"We simply attempt to be fearful when others are greedy and greedy when others are fearful."

This idea of starting with a phrase and twisting it from the opposite perspective was eloquently used by Dell Computer in ads they created to minimize the impact of one of IBM's most important marketing statements. For decades, IBM trained its salespeople to brag that,

"No one ever got fired for buying IBM,"

Dell gleefully countered with the line,

"But did anyone ever get promoted?"

Notice how taking the opposite of a statement can create a power statement, even if you're simply using it as a twist on your competitor's slogan?

These examples highlight the versatility chiasmus has in waking the brain while adding a level of credibility to an otherwise simple phrase.

As you can tell from the examples in this chapter, I love how powerful and versatile chiasmus can be in strengthening the impact of your power phrases.

Of course, I'm not the only one who loves chiasmus.

From Comedians To Presidents, Even Short Phrases Can Deliver Long Memories

In the entertainment industry, chiasmus has long been a staple of comedians.

- From Joey Adams – *"Never let a fool kiss you, or a kiss fool you."*

- From George Carlin – *"Don't sweat the petty things or pet the sweaty things."*

- From Randy Hanzlick – *"I'd rather have a bottle in front of me than a frontal lobotomy."*

How about this, from poet Dorothy Parker

– *"I'm not a writer with a drinking problem, I'm a drinker with a writing problem."*

And, of course, Mae West was the queen of chiasmus.

Not to let such an amazing tool go to waste, even American Presidents and important leaders have depended on chiasmus to help spice up their comments.

President John F. Kennedy loved chiasmus and used it often in his most famous speeches.

"Ask not what your country can do for you. Ask what you can do for your country."

"Let us never negotiate out of fear. But let us never fear to negotiate."

"Mankind must put an end to war, or war will put an end to mankind."

Britain's legendary Prime Minister, Winston Churchill, used chiasmus with joyful abandon...

"We shape our buildings, and afterward, our buildings shape us."

"I've taken more out of alcohol than alcohol has taken out of me." and

"I am ready to meet my maker; whether my maker is ready for the great ordeal of meeting me is another question."

Civil rights leader Martin Luther King Jr. regularly used chiasmus to make his profound points.

"We must build dikes of courage to hold back the flood of fear."

By presenting the phrase, *'dikes of courage,'* and following it with the opposite, *'the flood of fear,'* he created a striking statement that still resonates today, decades after he initially coined it.

Musicians often use chiasmus to help create hit songs.

From Oscar Hammerstein for Disney's Cinderella,

"Do I love you because you're beautiful? Or are you beautiful because I love you?"

And from Steven Stills of Crosby Stills and Nash,

"If you can't be with the one you love, love the one you're with."

Again, not only do phrases structured like this have increased power, they tend to be memorable for years, and in some cases, even centuries.

That's the power of chiasmus.

Here Are A Few Exercises To Help You Develop Your Own Chiasmus Phrases

What if you wanted to say that just because someone is quiet doesn't mean they're clueless?

What's the opposite of quiet... *'loud?'*

So, quiet people have a loud... what?

As writer Stephen King noted,

"Quiet people have the loudest minds."

The use of chiasmus elevates the power of his quote, doesn't it?

Okay, here's another one.

Let's say you're writing a book on personal development. You want your readers to understand that, to change their lives, they first have to change their beliefs. How can you explain that in a way that resonates?

Let's start by looking up cliches that include the word *'believe.'* Perhaps the best known is,

"I'll believe it when I see it."

Aha! This is an extraordinary statement that we could definitely play with through chiasmus!

Addressing this very concept, personal development coach and author Wayne Dyer twisted that phrase backwards for the title of his book,

"You'll see it when you believe it."

Think how powerful a statement this is. Only once you believe it will you begin to see it.

Not only did twisting that well-known phrase help propel his book to bestseller status, the phrase itself has been adapted for tee-shirts, mugs, quote libraries, and in talks by dozens of other top coaches.

Not bad for a title that probably took him less than an hour to develop.

Which begs the question, don't you want your own quotes and book titles to resonate this effectively with your audience?

If the answer is yes, then chiasmus may be the secret tool you'll want to explore. Here's how to begin.

Start by asking yourself, what do you want your listener or prospect to understand? Then, write the words that explain this.

Now, how can you reverse it using chiasmus?

Do this, and your words and ideas will suddenly become infinitely more influential.

From the words of playwright George Bernard Shaw,

"You see things that are, and ask, why?

I dream things that never were and ask, why not?"

Simply put, can you create profound and engaging statements like these?

Of course, you can!

Chapter Eleven

Trigger-Words

Vomiting On Your Presentation

The head of a training company that teaches English to people in other countries told me about a doctor she was working with at one of the hospitals in Vietnam. The doctor proudly explained how, as he and his wife were getting dressed for a major event, he complimented his wife with the new English he had been learning. With enthusiasm, he told his wife,

"You look beautiful, and you are stinky!"

He actually meant to tell her that she smelled wonderful. But what he didn't realize is that certain words, like *'stinky,'* are not meant as compliments.

So, here's my promise to you.

No more *'stinky'* presentations. That's the goal of this book, right?

Okay, how about this joke...

"What do lawyers and the word 'vomit' have in common?"

I don't even need a punchline to get a laugh from this question for many people. That's because certain words, like *'stinky'* and *'vomit,'* trigger an almost reflexive response in us.

Learning how to trigger reflexive responses in our audience is an integral part of what we're going through in this book. And the words you choose could be an especially valuable tool for this.

You may have heard the phrase, *"Don't think of pink elephants,"* knowing that the mere mention of *'pink elephants'* will make you think of them. In the same way, certain words will cause an engaging reaction in your listeners that could help elevate a point you're trying to make, or hurt it.

One of my daughters told me how she was at the park with her two little kids when her daughter's head collided with another child's, causing her to fall unconscious. After a moment, she was revived. But the shock of seeing his little sister unconscious was considerable for her son, and for good reason.

Later, trying to calm his fears, she told him his sister was fine, and it was just a freak accident. However, she then said something that caused a moment of sheer panic in him. She unwittingly said,

"Don't worry. Your sister wouldn't die from anything like this."

As soon as he heard the word *'die'* a look of shock came over him. My daughter suddenly realized that just mentioning that single word was enough to trigger anxiety in her little son.

In the same way certain words can cause anxiety in a little boy, your choice of certain trigger words can elevate the awareness in your prospect of something you want them to consider important.

First, there's an important point I'd like to make.

In a way, we are all partially sleep-walking through life.

We are so overwhelmed with information and have so many things on our minds that our brain is only partially engaged whenever someone tells us something, no matter how important they think it might be.

While we might honestly try to listen, our brain is thinking about what's for dinner, did I forget to do my taxes, did I forget to lock my car, how come my boss or client acted so strangely when I last talked to him, and a truckload of other issues. Plus, we're noticing the Coca-Cola glass on a nearby desk, a poster in the background, the strange shirt our co-worker is wearing, even the images on a nearby tv or computer, and more.

The point here is, even if you think they are listening intently to you, they're probably only half-listening to what you're saying.

But, introduce a trigger word to your conversation, and you can take hold of their full attention in ways that might be difficult otherwise.

A trigger word is a word that wakes up your listener's senses, at least for a moment.

Think of these words...

Stinky, Vomit, Racist, Rapist, Greedy, Naked, Outrage.

Strategically adding any of these to your conversation could boost the impact of what you say.

For example, in their tv and radio ads, Blu-Emu muscle cream, for relief from muscle pains and body aches, uses the memorable slogan:

"Blue-Emu works fast -- and you won't stink."

I remember first watching their ad featuring baseball Hall-of-Famer Johnny Bench and barely noticing it. Then, my attention was grabbed when he said their slogan. My brain asked, *"What did he just say?"*

Using the trigger word *'stink'* amplified their message enough that it "stuck in my brain like glue," as I know it did for millions of others who saw it.

Eve Ensler's play, *'The Vagina Monologues,'* became a hit off-Broadway in a large part because it has the word *'vagina'* in its title.

'Naked Juices' became hugely popular because they have the word *'naked'* in their name.

Politicians know this technique well. In recent years, words like *'racist,' 'sexist,'* and *'homophobe'* have been so overused that they have almost lost much of their value in identifying people who genuinely have these traits. And that's unfortunate.

Still, using the right trigger word can significantly improve your presentation's attention-getting power when you include it in your pitches.

Here are a few examples.

Try Not To Vomit By What I'm About To Tell You

Reps from a major financial services firm I was working with told me how easily they could find problems in insurance policies from certain of their competitors.

Using this to highlight a competitive advantage they had, I trained them to use this expression...

"I don't want you to vomit, but have you seen what's in this policy of yours?"

It took a while to get reps to use this phrase because it felt uncomfortable to say. Yet, once they started using it, not only did they find it easier to convert these prospects into buyers, but their presentations stopped feeling like blatant sales pitches. Instead, many of the reps told me how much fun it was to watch the expression suddenly change on a prospect's face whenever that word was used.

These reps also wanted a simpler way to impress on prospects how important it is to start setting aside as much money as possible as early as possible.

So, we developed a presentation explaining how fast cash gets used up if you don't invest it properly. It went something like this...

"Let's say you can save a million dollars by the time you're seventy. If you spend about $100,000-a-year, you'll be broke by the time you're eighty. Think about it. Who's going to hire you when you're eighty? Wal-Mart? I heard McDonald's is hiring old people. I guess they need someone to clean the vomit out of their parking lot."

Okay, this is harsh, for sure. And it took plenty of coaching to finally get reps using it. But once they did, you could see the wince on people's faces whenever they got to the phrase *"...clean the vomit out of the parking lot."*

Again, with a trigger word like that waking up the prospect, reps told me they felt more like teachers than salespeople.

And the increased results they enjoyed reflected the power of that.

It might sound incredible, but it worked in ways that surprised almost all the reps who used it!

Here's another trigger word that could be helpful.

How Worried Are You

Another trigger word that is often underused is, *'worry.'*

An ad I saw for a realty company started with the headline,

"Do you want top dollar for your home? Then hire the right agents."

To boost the power of their ad, a trigger word was needed. The reason is simple. People buy for emotional reasons more than logic, and this phrase focused more on the logical reason someone should hire them.

In my classes, I teach that you can grab your prospect's attention faster if you start with a legitimate compliment. Who doesn't like to be complimented?

Start with a compliment, then use the word *'worry,'* and you will often seize a greater degree of attention from your audience.

In this realtor's case, rather than saying,

"Do you want top dollar for your home? Then hire the right agents,"

...the power phrase becomes this...

"Do you have a beautiful home, but you worry that you won't get a great price when you sell it? Let us show you a simple way to solve this."

To turn their pitch into a powerful phrase that engages the mind, I started with a compliment, *"do you have a beautiful home,"* and then introduced the trigger word *'worry'* to heighten emotional engagement.

I used this same formula with an Internet marketing firm,

"Do you have a really terrific business, but you worry that you're not getting enough clients?"

...and with a child psychologist,

"Do you have a really terrific son, but you worry that he's not doing well enough in school?"

A change like this to a presentation might seem subtle, but the results of starting with a compliment and integrating a word that triggers emotion were unexpectedly greater than any of these clients expected, as it can be for you.

Choosing Words That Activate Emotion

I can't end this chapter without mentioning one of the most consequential, earth-shattering, monumental, weighty, and decisive elements of effective copywriting.

We often find ourselves using the same mundane words over-and-over again to describe our products and ideas, when amazing power words and phrases are so easily available at the end of our finger tips with a simple Google search, that elicit heightened emotional response in the people we are trying to sell.

Like these...

Instead of saying something is GREAT, why not call it,

extraordinary, spectacular, life-altering, cutting-edge, magical, revolutionary, remarkable, startling, awe inspiring, unprecedented, or *weirdly delightful.*

Instead of saying something is EASY, why not call it,

effortless, painless, idiot-proof, or *mindlessly simple.*

Remember, if you are trying to persuade someone, why not use the words and phrases that are actually designed to move us all emotionally?

Think about your own products and ideas.

Are you using *'trigger words'* to awaken prospects during your message?

What trigger word could you integrate into your presentation to make it more engaging and memorable?

From my experience with the myriad of people who have tried this, I've found that a trigger word introduced at the right moment into your presentation could improve the receptiveness of your prospect in valuable... and if they don't vomit, entertaining ways.

Chapter Twelve

Odd And Unexpected

You Might Die, But That's Okay

Using a word, phrase, or visual that's unexpected or odd can often help your product or idea "stick in your prospect's brain like glue," boosting your ability to persuade and sell in ways that might even surprise the most skeptical among us.

Take the experience of the obscure Canadian city that created a slogan so unusual, not only did their tourism revenues skyrocket, but pop icons Madonna and Mick Jagger of the Rolling Stones repeated it to their audiences of tens of thousands because they found it so... memorable.

As a kid growing up in Montreal, I remember hearing the name Regina, the capital of the province of Saskatchewan, and laughing as if someone had just said something totally inappropriate.

To a kid, it sounded like *'vagina,'* and that was enough to get us all laughing.

So, when someone in Regina needed to develop a slogan that would help boost their tourism, what do you think they did?

What would you do?

I guess it takes guts to do something like this, but the slogan they came up with was,

"Regina. It rhymes with fun."

Heck, besides being promoted all over their website and on tv and radio, they even had tee shirts and bumper stickers with that slogan.

Like most BRAIN GLUE phrases, it was engaging enough to drive droves of people to their website, where they could laugh while learning more about a city they had never before considered visiting.

After a few years, they killed the slogan, pretending they were surprised it might be offensive to some people. But not until it became the conversation piece for millions of people in Canada and the U.S.

Like many BRAIN GLUE tools, odd and unexpected phrases and slogans like this have the power to not only boost sales, but stick in your prospect's brain, even if they hear or see it only once.

That's the power of BRAIN GLUE!

Here's Why This Works So Well

One of the most important reflexes our brain has is its alertness to anything wrong or out of place. It's wired into our brains as a defense mechanism.

In the olden days, for survival, we needed to be able to spot a predator, even if it was hidden in a bush waiting to pounce. In modern times, this reflex is still deeply embedded in us. It helps us spot if a boss or client is displeased with something we say or do, by recognizing even a subtle hint of dissatisfaction in their voice, expression, or body language.

In a broader sense, this reflex catches things that are odd, out of place, or unexpected, focusing our attention like a laser on it.

From a persuasion standpoint, knowing how to tap this powerful brain reflex can be exciting and valuable, especially in a world where our message is competing against a constant barrage of information flooding towards our prospect every day. Knowing how to push through the barrage to seize our prospect's deepest level of attention is essential if we want to have even a prayer that our idea will be heard and accepted.

Think about it.

Wouldn't you love more people to open your emails, read your ads, watch your videos, and listen with deep interest to your pitches?

Unfortunately, without grabbing their attention right at the outset, it's generally not going to happen. Instead, your pitch will blend far into the background of your prospect's scanners, barely being noticed at all.

But, what if you could learn a skill that instantly activates your prospect's alert mechanisms, so they are not only made aware of your idea or product, but they want to know more?

In this chapter, you are about to learn how to activate the part of your prospect's brain that makes them hungry to learn more.

Are you ready?

This chapter is divided into five parts.

- Breaking a Pattern With An Unexpected Ending
- Creating Strange Combinations
- Altering Common Phrases
- Approaching the Line of Appropriateness, and
- Shocking Your Audience's Senses

Let's enter this world of brain waker-uppers that get people more attentive to your products and ideas.

Odd and Unexpected #1
Breaking a Pattern with an Unexpected Ending

Our brain has patterns already embedded in it, from nursery rhymes we've heard as a child to quotes and cliches we've encountered throughout our lives to experiences we've had. These patterns create an expectation of what's to come.

Being aware that our prospect is expecting something provides us an opportunity to surprise them with a different ending that awakens their senses.

Comedians love this.

"With great power comes great electricity bills."

"Twinkle twinkle little star, point me to the nearest bar."

"I want to change the world. But first, I have to change my underwear."

See how this works?

We take a phrase people already know, give them a surprise ending that they were not expecting, and suddenly, we've seized their attention, at least for a moment or two.

This works for book covers. Bestselling author Jenny Colgan named her book *'The Good, the Bad and the Dumped,'* taking advantage of the well-known movie title, *'The Good, the Bad and the Ugly.'*

This works for restaurants. J.D. Hoyt's Minneapolis steakhouse ran an ad saying, *"Mary had a little lamb. Frank ordered the porterhouse,"* taking advantage of the well-known nursery rhyme.

Mae West liked to say, *"Too much of a good thing can be wonderful."* Likewise, investor Warren Buffett explained his investment strategy with the line, *"Our favorite holding period is forever."* Both these quotes seize our attention by giving us surprise endings.

Cosmetics giant L'Oréal Paris ran a series of ads promoting the idea that more women should be hired in executive roles at major companies. One of their most noteworthy ads had five lipstick tubes on a red page with the unexpected headline,

"This is an ad for men."

Arby's restaurants wanted to promote the high-quality meats they offer. However, using the phrase, *"We offer a wide variety of meat,"* is too ordinary to grab anyone's attention. So, they created the phrase, *"Arby's. We have the meats."*

Strange as it may be, this slogan grabs attention while highlighting their most important assets, the quality, and variety of meats they offer.

The Wall Street Journal ran this headline,

"Money talks. We translate."

To explain the authenticity and ruggedness of their products, the Timberland shoe and sportswear company ran an ad with the headline,

"From the days when men were men. And so were the women."

Early in his career, songwriter Johnny Cash's unusually titled song, *"A boy named Sue,"* helped establish him as a major performing artist.

Each of these ads, quotes, book and song titles uses the element of surprise to bring attention to themselves and whatever they are offering.

So, how can you use the element of surprise to describe your own product or idea?

Introducing The One And Only

Let's say you were introducing one of the most powerful computers on the market. How would you come up with an attention-getting headline?

Well, the word *'power'* should probably be somewhere in your headline, right?

Let's search Google for quotes using the word *'power'* and see what comes up.

One of the first quotes that comes up is,

"Absolute power corrupts absolutely."

Okay. So, how could you twist that quote by giving it a surprise ending.

That's what the people at Apple did when they introduced a more powerful version of their Macintosh computer. The headline they came up with...

"Absolute power corrupts. Enjoy."

This headline grabs your attention while making its point that the new Macintosh is a more powerful computer than anything else that's out there.

Comedy Or Tragedy, You Choose

As a comedian, you could have great fun using unexpected endings.

Start by thinking of everything you see and hear on a typical day.

Standing near a fire extinguisher, you read, *"In case of fire, break glass,"* and suddenly, you have a starting point. In case of fire, what else can you break? And aha! You have it!

"In case of fire, break wind."

I include comedy in these explanations because there's a saying in the world of persuasion: *"If they're laughing, they're buying."* As we learned earlier, even mild laughter triggers oxytocin, which makes people more comfortable saying yes.

Plus, it's more fun if you can get your prospects to laugh, isn't it?

Laughter is certainly the best medicine. It triggers endorphins that make it easier for our bodies to fight off illness. It also makes persuading and selling easier.

Showing you how to construct jokes helps make it easier to understand how to construct your own power phrases, whether you use humor or not.

What Does A Mother Really Need

Okay. Let's say you want to create a Facebook page. You're an exhausted mother with kids who sometimes drive you crazy, so why not connect with other moms and parents like you. What might you call your Facebook page?

Mommy needs a moment to herself... Mommy needs a break...

Wait! I know what Mommy really needs!

"Mommy Needs Vodka!"

The *'Mommy Needs Vodka'* Facebook page has more than five million followers. Five million!

Including me!

Do you think having the name *"Mommy Needs Vodka"* has anything to do with her being able to amass such a large audience? Absolutely!

The first time I saw one of her posts, the page's name got me laughing.

The post was pretty funny, but the page's name got more of my attention. I had to join, especially when I saw some of the other posts on her page, which were consistent with what I expected.

Do you think I'm the only one who had this reaction?

"Mommy Needs Vodka" is a prime example of how saying something unexpected can generate far greater results for you, often without your even having to spend a nickel on advertising.

Of course, like *"Mommy Needs Vodka,"* you still need to have something they want once they visit you. A hot title will only bring people to your door. The quality of what you're offering will get them to come in.

Still, plenty of people with extraordinary products and content can't get people to even visit them. If you're one of those people, creating an unexpected title like *"Mommy Needs Vodka"* could solve this problem in incredible ways for you, often with little or no added investment.

There is another side to all this.

What Did He Say His Name Was

From comedian Carrot Top to ex-football great and sports commentator Dick Butkus to popcorn icon Orville Redenbacher to Arnold Schwarzenegger, people with unusual names have all learned the 'sticky' power of a memorable name.

Arnold was told his unusual name would be a liability in show business, but the opposite was true. Instead, his name, along with his thick Austrian accent, have proven to be his greatest assets in an industry where standing out from the crowd is tougher than most people realize.

Then there's Dick Butkus?

Tell me that name doesn't make you laugh. In case you missed it, his name is pronounced, Butt-Kiss. It's like Pussy Galore in the James Bond film Goldfinger. You'll definitely stand out from the crowd with a name like that.

Of course, your name doesn't have to be this outrageous or raunchy to grab attention. Sometimes the opposite is also true.

In the 1960s, filmmaker Sergio Leone developed low-budget spaghetti westerns that became massively popular and are still watched today. His most notable ones were with actor Clint Eastwood, including, *A Fistful of Dollars*, *For a Few Dollars More*, and *The Good, the Bad, and the Ugly.*

One of the elements that made these films so notable was Clint Eastwood's name in the film. Do you know what it was?

Actually, he had no name. He was known as, *'the man with no name.'*

Who ever heard of a movie where the star has no name? Have you ever heard such a crazy thing?

And yet, the fact that he was *'the man with no name'* helped propel these films to iconic status in the film world.

Sergio Leone seized on something everyone took for granted and gave us something unexpected. That's how classics are born.

Are You Ready To Be Scared

Understanding what an audience is used to doing and making them do something different will often wake up their brain and grab their attention.

For as long as theaters have been around, whenever someone would show up late for a movie, they would be let in to watch it if seats were still available.

Knowing this and wanting to bring greater attention to his movie Psycho, famed film director Alfred Hitchcock did something that had never been done before. He required movie theaters to not allow anyone in if they arrived late.

Technically there was a good reason. In a surprising twist, the main character gets killed off so early that audiences are shocked and confused in a way that had never been experienced before in a film.

Still, Hitchcock knew that altering the pattern of moviegoers with signs outside the theater and in their promotions would create an elevated sense of drama and expectation that there was definitely something different about this movie. And it worked. Massive lines formed to help turn Psycho into one of the most successful movies of its day.

That's what can happen when you make people do something unexpected.

Selling? No, Let's Buy Instead

Of course, this idea of breaking a pattern doesn't just work with names, phrases, and moviegoing. It can also be used to deliver a better result for something you're struggling with.

In the 1950s and '60s, Elmer Wheeler was considered the world's greatest salesman. He invented the phrase, *"Don't sell the steak – sell the sizzle,"* which is still taught today in sales and marketing classes.

Early in his career, Elmer sold and created newspaper ads for retailers. They initially complained that his ads brought people into their stores, but no one was buying. However, upon visiting these stores, he quickly realized the problem. People working in the stores were terrible at selling.

This led him to create America's first real sales-training program, teaching people in retail how to be more effective at getting visitors to buy through the words they used.

One of his greatest successes came from his work with Macy's department store in New York. Watching salespeople approach customers, he realized a certain kind of dance was involved. A salesperson would approach the customer and ask, *"May I help you,"* whereas the customer would say something like, *"No thanks. Just looking."* Then the salesperson would step away while the customer was left on their own to peruse items in the store.

Okay. What have we been talking about throughout this chapter? Understanding a pattern and then disrupting that pattern. Right?

So, what do you think Elmer Wheeler did with what he observed?

He came up with a different question for the salespeople to ask.

What if a salesperson would approach a customer, and instead of asking, *"May I help you,"* they instead asked, *"Could YOU help me?"*

Besides being unexpected, a question like this taps into most people's instinctive good nature by asking them for help.

Every salesperson who asked this question got a radically different response. Rather than the customer pushing them away, they would instead say, *"Sure, what can I help you with,"* attracting rather than repelling an interaction between the salesperson and the customer and ultimately boosting sales in the process.

Why Are You Calling

This reminds me of what Einstein used to say, that, *"The definition of insanity is doing the same thing and expecting a different result."*

Think of it for ourselves. How often do we find ourselves doing something that delivers marginal success at best, yet we continue doing it exactly the same way without ever changing?

If you ever find yourself doing something that doesn't work, maybe it's time to reexamine the process and consider ways to change it.

In work I did with the financial services company I mentioned previously, I was able to turn rejection into almost universal acceptance by applying this idea of altering a pattern people were used to.

As part of their training, I noticed the company had each rep calling an old schoolmate, a neighbor, or someone else who they hadn't talked to for years. As you can imagine, these proved to be uncomfortable calls that went like this. The rep would say something like,

"Hi, It's Joe Jones. We went to school together. Do you remember me?"

The person on the other end of the line would usually say yes. Then the rep would ask how their life was going, maybe a little about their family if they had one, and so forth.

Eventually, they would do what I call the 'toxic pivot.' They'd say,

"The reason I'm calling is, I have something that might be interesting to you, and I'm wondering if we could get together and discuss it."

Obviously, most of the people who were called would somehow pass on the offer, maybe saying something like, *"Why don't you send me something, and if I'm interested, I'll contact you,"* to end the call.

The problem with this approach is the person on the other end almost always knew the call wasn't out of the blue. They knew the rep was probably trying to sell them something. So, they'd wait until that 'toxic pivot' happened, where the real reason for the call was revealed, and use that to finally end the call.

Insane, isn't it, that they'd keep doing it the same way over and over again?

To the reps, this approach felt uncomfortable and disingenuous. Here they are in an industry that depends on trust, and they're starting by almost tricking the person into hearing their pitch. It felt like the rep didn't really care about their schoolmate's life to the prospect. All they really cared about was if they could give their pitch.

So, how do you solve a problem like this?

Instead of feeling like you're lying from the start, why not tell them why you're calling right at the beginning? In the first minute of the call, why not tell them,

"I'm calling because I want to sell you something."

Does this sound crazy? Here's what happened when I got them to change.

I sat with the first rep, an attorney who was also doing financial planning. He chose to call someone he had gone to law school with a decade earlier. Here's how his call started.

"Hi Amy, this is Gene. We went to law school together. Do you remember me?"

Her response, *"Sure."*

I could see his hesitation at using that line, so I leaned across the desk and whispered those words, which he reluctantly repeated.

"I'm calling because I want to sell you something."

How do you think she responded?

She laughed and asked,

"Okay. What do you want to sell me?"

He continued,

"First, I'd like to find out how you're doing, if that's okay."

She agreed, and they chatted for a few minutes, catching up on each other's lives. Then she asked,

"Okay. What do you want to sell me?"

As he explained, she commented that her financial rep had recently moved to the East Coast, and she actually needed someone. They chatted for a few more minutes, then set a time to meet in person, and hung up.

It doesn't always happen this smoothly, but Gene's results were dramatically better than anything he or anyone else in his group had achieved before.

So, what actually happened on this call?

First, he surprised his prospect by telling her the truth right from the start. From that moment forward, he felt more comfortable, and so did she, because the real purpose of the call was laid out honestly and quickly.

The point here is significant.

If what you do and say is working, stick with it.

But if it's not, recognize the pattern of what's happening and ask yourself if there's something you could say or do that would disrupt that pattern.

As it did for the reps I worked with, making just a slight change could deliver more dramatic results than you ever expected.

Remember, if you want different results, break the pattern and do something different.

If You Look Like Everyone Else, Maybe It's Time To Change

When Steve Jobs returned to Apple to run the company, the first product he created was the iMac, the first computer with a direct connection to the Internet.

But he did something else.

Instead of making his computer look dull and industrial gray in color like everyone else's, he wanted his product to stand out from the competition. So, he put translucent plastic covers on the backs so you could partially see inside at the electronics and gears that made it work. He also gave these plastic covers beautiful colors – blue, red, orange, green, and purple – something that had never been seen in computers before.

Not only did the original iMac become the most successful computer of its day, but it also helped establish Apple as a pioneer in the industry, an image that ultimately helped it become the most valuable company on the planet during his tenure.

This idea of making your product look different from everyone else's can also translate to service businesses.

Lou Wasserman, founder of MCA that eventually became Universal Studios, started his company as a talent agency in Hollywood representing directors, writers, actors, etc.

When other talent agents dressed casually, he required his agents to wear suits and ties. This created an image of professionalism while making them stand out visually from everyone else working at the studios.

Wasserman's company eventually became the most powerful agency in Hollywood, forcing the federal government to break it up. In a large part, their success was because of how his agents were perceived by Hollywood talent.

Taking a page out of Lou Wasserman's playbook, when I worked with biotech giant Amgen, I also wore suits and ties when everyone else dressed casually. Their senior managers told me that, like other tech giants, no one dressed up at Amgen and I didn't need to either. But I told them I preferred looking different than everyone there.

People who know me know I rarely wear a suit and tie. With Amgen however, it was a running joke between them and me. Someone would say, *"There's some guy with a suit wandering around the offices,"* and people would say, *"Oh, that Bond. He's working with our top managers."*

It was fun, but it also made a point. If you want to come across as a leader, the first thing you may consider is making your product or idea look different from everything that's out there.

Okay. So now that you understand the value of *Breaking the Pattern by Creating Unexpected Endings,* let's move on to the next power tool in this Odd and Unexpected Techniques chapter.

Odd and Unexpected #2
Creating Strange Combinations

Abbott & Costello. Lavern & Shirley. Penn & Teller. Beavis & Butt-Head. Rocky & Bullwinkle. The entertainment industry has seen plenty of dynamic duos.

But rapper *Snoop Dogg* and housewares maven *Martha Stewart?*

I'm not sure anyone saw this coming. In an act of promotional brilliance, putting two totally different celebrities from two radically different worlds together has helped propel them both to heights I don't believe either would have ever predicted.

Suddenly, Snoop is on the cover of women's magazines and is promoting products no other rapper would have been considered for, while Martha has aligned herself with companies like Canopy, the cannabis-related CBD company.

Recently, I was in a Trader Joe's food store and saw '19-Crimes' wine promoting Martha Stewart's Chardonnay White and Snoop's Red-Blend.

Wow! Who would have thunk it?

The idea of connecting two strangely different people or elements has proven to be a powerful way to bring attention to yourself and your products.

In Hollywood, Snoop and Martha are not the only strange couple to have expanded their success through an unexpected partnership. In 1982, Crooner Julio Iglesias and country legend Willie Nelson sang, *'To All the Girls I've Loved Before,'* in a beautifully strange ballad. The harmony was amazing, but the visual of a well-groomed city-slicker in a suit singing with a long-haired hippie-type made the collaboration noteworthy enough to expand their audiences and brands dramatically, all because they were such a strange combination.

Grinding Out Unexpected Combinations

How about combining your product with something unexpected in your ads?

Let's say you were trying to sell a heavy-duty food blender and wanted to demonstrate how strong your product was? What could you throw in the blender that would surprise everyone? How about an iPad, an iPhone, or Justin Bieber music disks?

This might sound ridiculous, but that's what Blend-Tech did in a series of low-budget videos that have become legendary in the history of YouTube, with virtually no promotion.

In one, the demonstrator takes a new iPad, folds it in half, and stuffs it into a blender. Then, he pushes the button as we watch it get ground into dust by this revolutionary blender.

The result?

That video alone has generated more than nineteen-million views on YouTube and millions in sales, all because they combined two things that you'd never expect to go together.

If you're like most people, you'd never expect an iPad in a blender. But introducing such an odd combination helped an unknown product achieve the kind of success most companies dream of, almost overnight and with practically no cost.

Strange Names That Sell

Let's say you were going to open a vegetarian restaurant. What would you call it?

Using this 'strange combinations' technique, you could start by asking yourself, what's something that definitely doesn't go with vegetarian food, or any food for that matter?

How about... dirt?

Amanda Cohen opened one of New York City's best vegetarian restaurants, calling it *'Dirty Candy.'*

I'm not sure it's the name I would have chosen for a restaurant, but apparently, New Yorkers disagree with me. Dirty Candy has emerged as one of the most popular vegetarian restaurants in the city. It certainly has a memorable name.

New Pig Corporation has become one of the largest rag and industrial cleanup suppliers in the world. Of course, having such a crazy name has helped.

It turns out *'pig'* is a nickname for rags, so I guess they figured, why not use that in our company name. After all, it will definitely be memorable. Plus, having their reps hand out pig-shaped hats to customers and even calling their catalog, *'The Pigalog"* would add fun to an otherwise serious product. And fun usually translates into profits, doesn't it?

In their case, it certainly does!

Okay. How about this?

Could a crazy name propel a book on an otherwise dull topic to massive success?

There are plenty of excellent books in publishing that have never reached enough of an audience to achieve success. The opposite is true for economist Steven Levitt and journalist Stephen Dubner. In 2005, they published their first book, melding pop culture with economics to turn a regularly dry topic into something more fun and attractive to the masses. They named it *'Freakonomics'* to let people know how different their handling of the topic would be.

And the rest, as they say, is history.

With such a different name and approach, their book sold more than four million copies and helped launch a multi-media franchise that includes regular segments on National Public Radio, a massively popular blog, and even a movie!

How about this?

Let's say you were creating a new tv show on a topic that already has plenty of competition. What name could you come up with that would attract an avalanche of viewers almost overnight, despite all the other shows on the same topic?

On cable tv, house flipping shows are immensely popular, where a team of contractors and interior designers buy a house in poor condition, transform it into something more beautiful and sell-able, and then sell it.

When the DIY channel wanted to launch its own house-flipping show into an already crowded market, they needed a different and memorable name.

In the industry, homes that are foreclosed on or abandoned are called *'zombies.'* So why not call the show *'Zombie House Flipping.'*

Giving their show such an unusual name, especially in an age where zombie tv shows and movies are popular, helped it become an instant success.

They created the strange combination of *zombies* and *house-flipping*.

At a time when dozens of major ice cream brands were fighting fiercely for consumer attention, Reuben Mattus came up with an ingenious way for his tiny brand to compete.

He believed that inventing a name that sounded foreign would make his ice cream seem exotic enough that people would want to try it, and would even be willing to pay a premium price for it. The strategy worked, helping propel his tiny brand to massive wealth for himself and his wife.

The name he came up with... *'Häagen-Dazs.'*

A Berkeley, California branding company needed an original name that inspired prospects to believe they were credible and creative enough to be hired to come up with product and brand names. So, they called themselves,

'A Hundred Monkeys.'

This name is clever because the number – *'a hundred'* – implies they have plenty of employees, while calling themselves *'monkeys'* makes them appear unique and even a little gutsy and playful. With clients like Google's parent, Alphabet, I'm guessing this naming strategy worked for them.

So, how about you? From a brainstorming standpoint, what are some of the strangest things you could combine your product or idea with, that would surprise your prospects?

Why It's Important To Deliver More Than Just A Great Title

I recently saw an ad for a book and, after I laughed my pants off, decided to include a description of it here. The book is *'No, I can't Make Your Wife Disappear – A Magician's Guide to a Magical Marriage.'*

The idea of combining magic with marriage counseling is a terrific way to make it stand out from the crowd of books on relationships. However, when I read the book's description, I was disappointed. I realized it didn't reinforce the subject described in the title and subtitle.

Rather than illustrating what *magic* and *relationships* could have in common, it actually sounded pretty conventional and thus, made the title seem gimmicky rather than relevant.

I'm sure it's a great book, but here's a warning.

Your title may be fantastic at grabbing attention. But if your book or product itself doesn't deliver on what the title promises or implies, you will fail, even with an incredible attention-getter.

However, once you do have a good product, emotional triggers like these could help catapult it beyond your competitors in this overcrowded marketplace, as it has for so many others.

Odd And Unexpected #3
Altering Common Phrases

Have you ever heard the expression, "Waiter, there's a fly in my soup?"

I remember reading an article about a decade ago in the Wall Street Journal titled,

"Waiter, there's a rat in my soup, and it's delicious."

The article talked about how rats are commonly eaten in China and came with a warning. Don't eat more than two at a time because you'll get nose bleeds because it thins your blood.

Yuck!

I was attracted to this article, and I remember the title more than a decade later because they took that phrase, *"Waiter, there's a fly in my soup,"* and twisted it.

Slightly altering common phrases like this tends to grab attention and make them memorable.

Here are a few more examples.

Great Minds Think Unalike

When Utah was looking for a slogan to help boost the number of winter visitors to their state, the first thing that came to mind was the fabulous winter sports, ski hills, and snow-covered mountains that line the state. I'm guessing that, therefore, the slogan they wanted to come up with had to include the words *skiing* or *snow.*

If we look for words that rhyme with *'snow,'* one that comes up is the word, *'show.'* Looking up quotes that use the word *'show'* and up pops the phrase, *"The greatest show on earth."*

Wow! How about,

"Utah: The greatest snow on earth."

This has proven to be highly effective and memorable as a slogan by twisting a common phrase that's already embedded into our minds.

In its ads, British newspaper, *'The Times of London'* took the phrase, *"great minds think alike,"* and twisted it into,

"Great minds think unalike."

This terrific headline defines its readers as creative with such a brilliantly simple twisting of a well-known phrase.

The James Bond film *"Live and Let Die"* sticks in our brains because it twists the commonly known phrase, *"Live and let live."*

Investment firm T.D. Ameritrade's popular trading platform is called *"Think-or-Swim,"* twisting the phrase *"Sink-or-Swim,"* to create an instantly memorable and meaningful name for their product.

"Thank You for Smoking" became the funny and attention-getting title of the satirical black comedy about a lobbyist for the tobacco industry, taking advantage of the well-known signs in restaurants and public venues that say, *"Thank you for not smoking."* Using a title that twists such a well-known phrase helped turn the film and the book into ready-made classics.

Porsche loves this idea of twisting common phrases to bring attention to the most outstanding features of their cars. The headline, *"Separates Le Mans from Le Boys,"* brings attention to the racecar positioning they consider important, while their headline, *"Unclogs Major Arteries,"* helps establish an intellectual feel for their car brand.

In one of their most memorable ads, car maker Land Rover used the line, *"Our return policy is simple. YOU will return,"* highlighting the off-road feature of their vehicles.

Comedian Johnny Carson stretched the common phrase, *"Money can't buy you love,"* into the seriously funny yet prescient comment,

"Money can't buy you friends, but if you have enough money, you can rent your friends."

A comedian who will remain anonymous, probably because they don't want to be remembered for this, twisted William Shakespeare's quote, *"A rose by any other name would smell as sweet,"* into this,

"A fart by any other name is just as sweet."

I'm not sure I agree with this sentiment, but at least it demonstrates how versatile this idea of altering a common phrase can be.

Each of these examples connects because they tap something that's already embedded in our brains. Mentally and emotionally, we know how the phrase is supposed to work. When it doesn't go as expected, our senses are suddenly heightened and engaged in ways a simple phrase cannot deliver.

Odd And Unexpected #4
Approaching... and Crossing the Line

The name of the FCUK clothing and homeware stores grabs our attention because it looks like a misspelling of a swear word when it actually represents something more innocent. When the U.K. -based French Connection chain expanded to America, emails between the branches referred to their head office as FCUK, meaning French Connection, U.K.

Eventually, someone with a lot of guts recognized the attention-grabbing appeal and changed the company's name to FCUK.

This highlights an interesting category in our 'Odd and Unexpected' chapter. How coming close to the line of raunchiness is definitely a way to grab instant attention for yourself and your product, if you're willing to step beyond standard convention.

How Close Should You Come To The Edge

Carey Smith's *'Big Ass Fans'* company sold for an incredible $500 million dollars after a little more than fifteen years in business. Do you think the company would have grown that big and that fast if he'd had a more conventional name? I don't think so.

How about *'In-N-Out Burgers?'* Who would ever name their burger joints *'In-N-Out?'* Isn't that a sexual reference? The double entendre combined with a great product has propelled this family-owned California fast-food chain into a massive success in the Western U.S. Having a name that comes close to the line has helped them compete head-to-head with the majors in a way that has made them rich beyond their wildest dreams.

How about *'Hooters,'* with more than 400 restaurants worldwide? Their logo of an owl implies an owl's hoot was the source of their name. But everyone knows it refers to slang for a woman's breasts. So although the main feature of their restaurants is the harmless *'Hooters Girls'* – young women waitresses in white tank tops and orange runner's shorts – the implied raunchiness of their name has even attracted people to protest against building a Hooters in their communities. Still, that name has helped them build a massively successful brand, needing almost nothing more than a building sign with their name on it as promotion.

How about this?

Let's say you wanted to publish a series of books for beginners on just about any topic, with a beginner-friendly format that included plenty of illustrations, humor, and jokes combined with state-of-the-art information. What would you call it?

- The *'For Beginners'* books?

- The *'Starter Guides'* series of books?

You'd never consider insulting your audience, would you? I mean, why would you ever call your series of books *'For Dummies?'* And yet, with more than 200 million books already published, it has become one of the most lucrative brands in publishing. All because they decided to 'approach the line' by giving their brand a name that grabs attention by practically insulting anyone who would consider buying it.

The movie *'My Big Fat Greek Wedding'* and the cable tv show *'Queer Eye for the Straight Guy'* became instant successes in a large part because they had names that approached the line of acceptability.

Is it okay to spank a woman?

What if you created a revolutionary body-slimming undergarment for women made of spandex and wanted to shorten the word to *'Spanx'®?* Should it matter that it sounds like something inappropriate to do to a woman?

Actually, I guess not.

For Sara Blakely, her trademarked invention, along with a name that slides close to the edge of appropriateness, helped turn her into the youngest female billionaire ever in America.

How about using the word *'ugly'* to describe your product? That wouldn't be okay, would it?

In advertising, who would ever believe that calling your product *'ugly'* would be a great marketing strategy. Yet ad legend Bill Bernbach did just that when he promoted the Volkswagen Beetle to the world. His ads, calling the distinctive-looking vehicle a *'lemon,'* proclaiming that, *"Ugly Is Only Skin Deep,"* and promising, *"The 1970 V.W. will stay ugly longer,"* helped propel it into one of the best-selling cars of all time.

I'm not suggesting you insult your audience or belittle the product you're selling. But there's no ignoring the promotional power of a product name or description that approaches the line.

Yes, it takes guts to do something like this. But approaching the line could definitely give you an unexpected edge in this overcommunicated world.

Odd And Unexpected #5
Shocking Your Audience's Senses

As a young kid in advertising, I remember seeing a pretty startling ad for a graphic artist trying to get a job on Madison Avenue. It was a single page with an image of a dog whose face is half white and half black, with a gun to his head. The caption read,

"Hire me, or this dog dies."

Later, National Lampoon magazine had the same image on the cover of their magazine, with the headline,

"If you don't buy this magazine, we'll kill this dog."

I'm not suggesting you create ads this shocking, but it is noteworthy that doing something shocking that makes you stand out from the crowd could be valuable in this highly competitive world.

Early in their rise to becoming a major footwear company, Timberland ran a memorable series of ads with somewhat shocking headlines. In one, the headline read,

"Your eyes are frozen, your skin has turned black, you're technically dead. Let's talk boots."

In another, highlighting the authenticity of their moccasins, their ad with an image of a North American Indian chief had the headline,

"We stole their land, their buffalo, and their women. Then we went back for their shoes."

I'm not sure an ad like this would pass muster in today's ultra-sensitive woke environment. But these ads do highlight the power of shocking your audience into noticing you and your message.

Of course, raising the emotion level of your prospects this high could backfire, so be careful.

Still, done skillfully, the idea of shocking your audience into awareness for your product or idea could deliver a ready buyer that's ultra-motivated by the message you are trying to communicate.

Applying 'Odd and Unexpected' to Your Own Messaging

Throughout this chapter, we've explored a wide variety of ways to grab your prospect's attention.

From unexpected endings that break a pattern to creating strange combinations of words and images to twisting well-known phrases and more, hopefully, you will be inspired to uncover an engaging name and description for a product or idea you are trying to sell.

To get you going, start by asking yourself these questions:

- What's the name of your product, service, or idea?
- How could you make it the opposite of what people expect?
- How could you present your product or idea in a way that surprises people while highlighting the main feature or benefit your product or idea offers?

Initially, don't be concerned by how crazy your ideas might be. Brainstorming through extreme examples could be the best catalyst to uncovering your own best ideas.

With these answers as a starting point, transforming whatever your idea or product is into a powerful mind-magnet that glues your prospect's brain to whatever you are selling could be easier than you expect.

Chapter Thirteen

Rejecting To Attract

No, You Can't Have That

Warning. This section is not for all audiences.

Just kidding.

Actually, this is the chapter where we explore how telling someone they can't have something will often make them want it even more.

I recently saw an ad with the headline,

"Warning – The following Photos Are Unedited And Not Intended For All Audiences."

Do you think anyone clicked on the link? I'm betting many people did, and continue to, as it keeps reappearing in retargeting ads.

How about this?

Do you think it's possible that putting a warning label on certain products will increase their sales?

That's what happened with Parental Advisory Labels that, since 1990, have been posted on music albums to warn parents of strong language and sexual or violent content. The warning labels became a magnet for many who self-identified as rebels. These kids and adults go out of their way to buy music with these labels as a status symbol to show they are cool.

I'm not saying you should put a warning label on your product. But defining who shouldn't buy your product may help strengthen your pitch and boost your sales.

Does 'No' Sometimes Mean 'Yes'

Tell someone they can't have something, and they'll want it even more!

This may not always be the case, but it applies more often than many of us may realize.

It's how Bernie Madoff was able to screw dozens of the biggest celebrities and most prominent people in the world to invest in his fraudulent Ponzi scheme.

Let's say movie director Steven Spielberg was told by a friend that investing in Bernie's fund was incredible, that he'd make more money here than anywhere else. Spielberg would probably approach Bernie and say he wanted to invest. Using *'negative'* selling, Bernie would say,

"Sorry, I'm not taking any more investments."

Spielberg would probably respond with something like,

"Can't you make an exception?"

"Sorry."

"But I'm Steven Spielberg! And I have plenty I can invest!"

"Nope, I don't care if you're the Pope. And frankly, you'd have to have at least ten million dollars to invest for me to even consider you."

"I can do that. I can even do fifteen if that helps."

"Sorry, I can't. If I let you invest, I'd have plenty of others screaming at me and asking why I let you invest when I didn't let them."

"I won't tell anyone. It'll just be between you and me."

"I shouldn't do this!"

"Please, let's do this."

"Oooooookay, but if you tell anyone, I'll throw your money right back at you so fast that you won't know what hit you. Understand?"

"Yup. Thank you. You won't be sorry."

As ridiculous as this sounds, it's exactly how Madoff was able to swindle many of the world's most famous and prominent people out of millions of dollars of their money.

This is called reverse selling, where the seller acts like a buyer. Rather than saying, *"Please buy from me,"* they say the opposite,

"You need to tell me why I should take your money."

This works because we buy for emotional reasons, sometimes backing it up with logic. Activate the emotional centers of someone's brain, and you can often get them to do amazing things. Even buy from you.

We all know that introducing scarcity to a sales pitch will increase the number of people who buy. Tell someone there are only a few left, and suddenly it creates a sense of urgency in the prospect. Not always, but often enough to make a difference.

But there's more.

The Opposite Of What People Expect

Have you ever heard the hit song *"I'm not in love"* by 10 CC? He says, *"I'm not in love,"* but it's obvious that the opposite is true. Denying that he's in love is a ruse to try and fool her and maybe himself too.

In marketing, telling someone you don't want them can sometimes be a great way to get them to want it even more. Clothing maker Patagonia sold a surprisingly large number of jackets with the headline,

"Don't buy this jacket."

The angle they used was, you shouldn't buy something you don't need. This example helps demonstrate the power of *'takeaway'* selling and highlights a common mistake in marketing. Marketers often fear explaining to a prospect who they're NOT interested in selling to, when in reality, there are always people who are not ideal prospects.

I worked with a Unishippers franchisee who wanted help selling his services to manufacturers and distributors that use UPS and other shipping services. I asked who his ideal prospect was, and he quickly answered, *"Anyone who ships products."*

I disagreed and spent time chatting with him until he admitted his ideal prospect was anyone who spends five thousand to fifty thousand a month on shipping. Less than that probably isn't worth the effort, while someone who spends more than fifty-thousand a month can probably get a better price working directly with UPS and other shippers. But less than fifty thousand, his company could usually get much better deals for them.

Altering his pitch so it started by explaining this changed everything. Here's what he now said,

"I'm looking for people who spend five to fifty thousand a month on shipping. More than that, you can probably get a better deal yourself. But between five and fifty thousand, we can usually save you a ton of money. I'd like to show you how. Could we set up a short meeting? I think you'll find it helpful."

Admitting his service was not for everyone made him come across as more honest and made prospects more willing to listen to his pitch, boosting his sales while reducing the stress he felt with the selling process.

So, here are a few questions that could help boost the power of your pitch.

- Who is your ideal buyer, and how are they different from everyone else?
- Who is not an ideal client, and how are they different from everyone else?
- Why would you *not* want to take someone's money?
- Who do you definitely *not* want as a client?

Explaining this to your prospect could make it much easier to persuade and win clients.

Chapter Fourteen

Sense Elevation

What's That Smell

Jaw dropping, eye opening, sticky, smelly...

What do these words and phrases have to do with this chapter? Everything, actually.

We're about to enter the realm of the five senses. Sight, smell, sound, taste and touch.

In this chapter, you're going to discover how injecting an added 'sense' to your explanation and presentation can significantly amplify the emotional engagement with your prospects in a way that almost instantly boosts their receptiveness to what you are proposing.

Sense elevation is all around us in ways we may not recognize because they are so commonplace.

I remember watching a hilarious video of new dads trying to avoid vomiting while they changed their infants' diapers. Pulling the diaper open, they'd suddenly be overcome by a smell that so overwhelmed their senses, it activated an uncontrollable urge to heave while they were trying to perform one of the most basic of parenting tasks.

Hopefully, your own presentations won't make your prospects want to heave. Hopefully, they won't want to vomit as they read your words or hear you speak.

However, introducing an additional and maybe even unexpected sense into your presentation will often heighten your prospect's engagement with your message in a way that makes it easier to get them to buy. That's what we will be addressing in this chapter.

Let's begin.

>> CAN YOU 'SMELL' THAT? <<

Smell is important to the French, with Grasse, France, known as the world's perfume capital. So, it's no surprise that just before going into a major battle, French general Napoleon sent a note to his darling Josephine that read,

"Home in three days. Don't bathe."

My students will often voice a 'Yuck' when they hear this. But at a time in history when body odor may have also been the ultimate aphrodisiac, addressing the scent of his lover might have been a little more commonplace than most historians will suggest.

For students of history and even readers of this book, highlighting smells associated with certain pungent or savory tones could make your message significantly more vivid and appealing.

Could Certain Smells Make People More Likely To Buy

High-end home sellers will often bake bread in the oven, install a real Christmas tree during the holidays, or light the fireplace during cold months to fill the house they're trying to sell with scents that activate positive emotions.

But did you know the smell of certain flowers, especially lavender, can make it easier to get someone to buy from you?

Yes, it's true. Lavender reduces anxiety and stress, making people more comfortable trusting you, especially if you are trying to get them to invest in financial assets like insurance or securities.

The impact of these kinds of scents on buying behavior is why so many grocery outlets have flowers near the front of their stores. Numerous studies have indicated that sales increase when people can smell certain floral scents.

One of America's leading toy companies conducted an experiment. Without advertising it, they infused half their plastic fire trucks with chocolate smell and the other half without. Not surprisingly, the ones with the chocolate scent far outsold the regular ones. Afraid they would be accused of trying to manipulate kids, they ceased the experiment. Still, their experience demonstrated the incredible power smell could have on buying.

One of the secrets to the success of Mrs. Field's Cookie Shops is their baking small batches of cookies and venting the baking smell into the malls where they are located. From the beginning, Debbie Fields knew smell could be a powerful sales tool for her shops.

With Duncan' Donuts shops blanketing many of South Korea's cities, the nation's transit authority came up with an interesting experiment. Every time the Duncan' Donuts jingle played on the radio, they would pump coffee aroma through the ventilation system to bus passengers. The result? There was a 16% spike in visitors to shops near the bus stops and almost a 30% increase in coffee sales at those same shops.

These examples highlight the impact smell can have on boosting sales.

Companies like International Flavors and Fragrances have built massive fortunes based on their ability to duplicate just about any scent and apply it to everything from car interiors to products to buildings and more.

Open the door of a 1977 Ford on a used car lot, and suddenly the smell of a Mercedes-Benz or Rolls Royce interior could be flooding your nostrils. *New Car Essence* is one of the many products available from IFF's portfolio of marketing smells designed to make selling a tad easier.

IFF even experimented with New York's Sanitation Department by having them mix the scent of green grass into its street-washing water. Sadly, the effects didn't last long. But even the trashiest of streets smelled like a walk along a mountain stream for a short while.

These are examples of where specific smells affect us. But here's something most people don't realize. You don't always need the scent itself to deliver the result you want. Often, just mentioning words that describe a smell can significantly impact people's willingness to buy your product or idea.

Like alliteration, rhyme, and chiasmus that ignite multiple parts of the brain, adding words that unexpectedly describe a smell, taste, touch, and yes, even a smell can engage those same parts of the brain, creating a mentally hyper-involved interaction between your prospect and what you are presenting.

Don't believe it? Consider these sense-heightening phrases that have helped generate billions in sales and in many ways, have transformed the way we buy certain products.

Could Simply Mentioning 'Smell' Be Enough To Boost Results

When this chapter started, did you notice a strange smell? Phew!

Introducing the idea of smell to something where smell is not customarily associated can be incredibly powerful. Ever hear the phrase,

"The sweet smell of... victory!"

What exactly does victory smell like? Sweaty clothes? I don't know, but focusing the mind on the idea of victory's smell adds an unexpected power to that phrase, doesn't it?

Remember the movie *'Apocalypse Now,"*

"I love the smell of napalm in the morning... It smells like... victory."

Introducing words related to smells adds a level of vividness that engages the exact parts of the brain that make persuasion easier. In fact, smell may be the most powerful of the senses because it's the most closely linked to memory and emotion.

My wife likes telling the story of a boyfriend she had in high school. His mother accidentally burned rubber in the clothes dryer. His clothes always smelled like burnt rubber from that moment forward, nauseating her and ultimately ending their relationship.

Now, whenever she hears the word *'boyfriend,'* she thinks of burnt rubber.

Luckily, I don't smell like burnt rubber, so our relationship has lasted... at least for now.

That's the impact of smell, but it also explains how mentioning smell can trigger interesting emotions in our audience.

Try Not Stinking Up The Room With Your Ads

Let's say you're a plumber and you came up with something people want – a $99 deal to unclog just about any drain regardless of the complexity of the problem. You know most plumbers charge a minimum fee just to come out and evaluate the situation, whether they can fix it or not. Plus, they won't even give you a specific price until they evaluate the cause of the problem.

So, you believe your offer – of $99 to unclog just about any drain – will help overcome much of the frustration most consumers have, possibly generating an avalanche of income if you could somehow let people know about what you're offering.

To reach the largest number of people the quickest, you've decided to spend money on radio ads.

However, you know that even with a great offer, you'll need an attention-grabber to make your ad stand out from the crowd, so people notice and remember your pitch.

What would you do?

Here's something many marketers don't realize. Whether it's on tv, on the radio, in an email, on a social post, in a newspaper, or wherever, even if you have an incredible offer, the ability to break through the clutter of all the ads trying to scream out and grab the audience's attention can be a real challenge.

That's why coming up with a gimmick or technique that gets your message heard and remembered could skyrocket your results even more than simply having a great offer, even if your offer is outstanding.

To grab attention, you could start by introducing *smell* into your ad. That's certainly not something many people are doing on the radio, are they?

But how could you use it for a plumber?

Let's start by asking a simple question. What smells are associated with plumbing?

Smelly toilets that overflow. That's something you could use. What else?

Mold that smells. What else?

Let's think more deeply about this. What's a smell you could mention that would be so unexpected, it would rise up through the noise and grab everyone's attention in a way no other ad is doing?

How about mentioning *'stinky plumbers?'*

After all, we know the *'plumber's crack'* story, where the plumber's butt hangs out as he leans under a sink to fix something. The worst plumbers show up stinky and sweaty, with dirty clothes, and with that plumber's crack hanging out. So why not give your company the slogan, *'The smell-good plumber,'* and see what happens?

That's what Orange County, California-based Mike Diamond Plumbing did.

'The smell-good-plumber' has become one of Southern California's most lucrative plumbing businesses on the strength of his radio ads combined with an offer that stands out from the crowd. Mike's biggest problem is finding enough plumbers to service all the customers his ads attract.

There's also another benefit to having such a memorable slogan. The phrase, *'the-smell-good-plumber,'* sticks in the brain like glue. So, even if someone is not ready to call a plumber yet, whenever they're finally ready, Mike's *'smell-good-plumber'* will be top-of-mind because of that funky, smell-based slogan.

By the way, if you go to Google and type the words, *'the smell good plumber,'* guess what comes up? Mike Diamond, of course. He was smart enough to buy the domain as well.

See how adding *'smell'* to your ads could boost engagement with your audience?

Like Blue-Emu's arthritis pain-relief cream that promises *"fast relief... and you won't stink,"* introducing smell to your ads could significantly boost their effectiveness.

Of course, smell isn't the only sense you can use to boost the power of your marketing and selling.

>> CAN YOU ‘HEAR’ THAT? <<

When Steve Jobs introduced his first Macintosh computer on stage in 1984, he demanded that as soon as he pulled it out of a bag and revealed it to his audience, the computer would blurt out the words...

“Hello, I’m Macintosh. It sure is great to get out of that bag.”

By having his computer simulate a robotic voice, he demonstrated to the world how the future of humankind had just arrived. At a time when computers didn’t talk, and robots were science fiction, Jobs knew that adding sound would heighten the impact of his revolutionary product launch.

And he was right.

Although internal battles got Apple to struggle for more than a decade following that launch, the power of the image he created with his talking computer resonated strongly with his audience. It was so strong that it ultimately helped turn customers into raving fans who would stand outside its stores in massively long lines, so they could be among the first to own anything new his company created.

Real Sound Versus Describing A Sound

Like Steve Jobs, many marketers recognize the importance of sound in helping build a solid fan base and creating high-impact messages.

Remember the anti-drug tv ads with the slogan,

“This is your brain on drugs, any questions?”

If you listened to any of their ads, the exaggerated sizzling sound of the frying pan boosted the power of their message to high-engagement levels.

In their tv ads, the UroLift medical treatment for enlarged prostrates exaggerated the sound of running water. They understood how hearing running water ignites a need to go to the bathroom for many. So, they knew raising that sound in their ads would heighten the impact of their message, and it did.

Radio ads for Mike Diamond Plumbing always have a harp strum whenever the words, *'the smell-good plumber,'* are mentioned, strengthening the memorability of their ads.

Harley Davidson motorcycles have such a distinct sound that the company tried to get a patent on it. When that didn't work, they tried to get it trademarked to prevent competitors from using the same sound with their bikes. Although that also ultimately failed, the sound of their bikes remains their iconic signature. Even blindfolded, people can still tell the sound of a Harley.

Companies like Rolls Royce and Mercedes spend plenty to ensure that something as simple as the sound of a door closing is consistent with the image they are trying to project. Like Harley, they understand that sound is essential in creating an image for your product.

So yes, having or using a unique sound could effectively strengthen the connection people have to your brand or message.

In my exploration of BRAIN GLUE, I also discovered how even the mention of sound in your pitches and headlines could boost the impact of your selling.

Plop Plop, Fizz Fizz, Oh, What A Technique It Is

In the 1960s, as a remedy for acid indigestion and stomach pain, Alka Seltzer was struggling. Their scientists eventually discovered that a single tablet wasn't enough to relieve the pain most consumers felt; they needed two tablets. But how do you highlight the importance of using two tablets?

The outstanding feature of Alka Seltzer has always been the dropping of a tablet into water where it fizzes while you drink the bubbling liquid. So, to let everyone know that two tablets were needed, they came up with a remarkably successful marketing campaign that used the sound of the fizzing tablets as their primary attention-getter, with,

"Plop plop, fizz fizz – oh, what a relief it is."

The fact that the slogan also used rhyme helped make it even more memorable.

One of their ads went even further by having the sound of food being eaten in the slogan followed by the sound of the Alka Seltzer tablets, with,

"Chomp Chomp, Sip Sip, Plop Plop, Fizz Fizz."

What's interesting about this attention-elevating technique is, it worked for print ads just as well as with tv and radio.

What's also important is how the phrase doesn't just give you the product's sound. The phrase, *"...oh, what a relief it is,"* also reminds you of the benefit the product promises.

Sales took off like gangbusters for Kellogg's Rice Krispies breakfast cereal when they highlighted the sound it made when milk is added, with the slogan,

"Snap Crackle Pop, Rice Krispies."

Verizon grabbed our attention with one of the most memorable phrases in phone advertising. To promote how their signal is stronger in more locations than their competitors, you might ask what *sound* does someone hear when the signal is lost?

It's usually someone asking,

"Hello? Are you still there? Can you hear me?"

To promote this, they came up with the ultra-memorable slogan,

"Can you hear me now?"

The same way Verizon did it, choosing a commonly used phrase as your slogan could anchor your own product or idea to it, so from that moment forward, any time someone hears or uses those words, your product or idea will come to mind.

Is Your Ad Making Funny Sounds

In an ad for Rolls Royce, one of the world's most luxurious car brands, legendary ad man David Ogilvie came up with a memorable headline that highlighted the unique silence of the ride,

"At sixty miles an hour, the loudest noise in this new Rolls Royce comes from the electric clock."

Most advertisers would simply have said the ride is silent. But introducing the sound of the electric clock heightens the vividness of the message, doesn't it?

Ads for Porsche sports cars also use sounds that heighten the power of their ads.

Imagine if you were creating an ad for an incredible sports car. What sound would you use? Maybe you could imagine your car screaming down the road. The word *'screaming'* comes to mind and could be great fun to include in a car ad. But how?

Maybe it's not the car that's screaming but the driver.

"After a long day at the office, it helps to go off by yourself and scream."

Porsche came up with this headline above a photo of one of their cars, creating a memorable, almost iconic ad that resonates with their audience. See how that works?

Ads like this, that add a sound to their headline, can deliver a heightened engagement with your audience that helps strengthen the message you are trying to convey.

So, how can you introduce sound into your explanation of the product or idea you are selling?

>> CAN YOU 'SEE' THAT? <<

Have you ever heard the expression, *"Seeing is believing?"*

I'll go a step further. *"Seeing is understanding!"*

What your prospect sees through their eyes and through the words you use can have a huge impact on how they perceive the value of what you're offering or proposing.

- High-end retailer Tiffany's trademarked a distinctive robin's-egg-blue color for their bags and boxes.
- Coca-Cola designed its bottles to mimic Marilyn Monroe's sexy shape.
- Michael Jackson used a single silver glove to help establish a unique visual image for himself.

- Marketing guru Seth Godin established his bald head and yellow-framed glasses as an iconic image that sets him apart visually from other marketers.
- Schneider Trucking has established the Omaha-orange color for all their trucks and trailers because it's highly distinctive, visible from afar, and helps emphasize their focus on safety.

Each of these people and businesses understood the value of creating a unique visual image to help differentiate themselves from the alternatives. They also understood the power of visual landmarks – how certain images and colors can activate specific emotions and expectations that could help or hurt the impression they want to portray.

Studies have shown how someone in a doctor's white coat can be more believable and trusted than someone in torn jeans.

Silicon Valley-based Elizabeth Holmes was able to con investors out of almost half-a-billion dollars, in part by dressing in a black turtle-neck shirt to resemble Apple's iconic founder, Steve Jobs.

By themselves, this type of image management may not be enough to push a buyer across the finish line. But in concert with other elements and with a great offer, it's often enough to get you the result you are seeking.

Wanna See Something Amazing

When we talk about trying to persuade someone, almost nothing can beat a demonstration to make your point.

That's what Electrolux did.

To prove their vacuum cleaner was one of the most powerful available, they created a video of their Intensity vacuum lifting five bowling balls in a large tube, making the point,

"If it's strong enough to lift five bowling balls, think of all the dirt it could lift out of your carpets."

To demonstrate the power of their food blender, the creator of Blend-Tech's food processors ground an iPad to dust on video, supported the promise,

"If that's what it does to an iPad, think how well it could grind just about any food you put in it."

To demonstrate the purity of his company's motor oil, one of America's top oil salesmen would drink from a container in front of his client, grossing the prospect out while reinforcing his claim.

That's why infomercials built on product demonstrations have proven so effective.

So, how about you? Do you use a demonstration in your ads and presentations?

Personally Engaging Your Prospect

At their annual conference, the top rep for PPG glass, the maker of safety glass, including that for car windshields, was asked how he became so successful.

He explained that he'd show up to the client's office armed with a piece of PPG's glass and a ball-peen hammer. Then, he'd shatter the glass in front of the prospect, demonstrating how the thin layer of plastic on each side prevented the shards from flying out of the glass.

Shocking as this demonstration was, it made a dramatic point that helped him close valuable sales.

The following year, the company armed all their reps with glass and ball-peen hammers. Yet, the same rep far exceeded the others in results. When asked what he did differently, he responded,

"This time, I gave the hammer and the glass to the prospect, and let him shatter it."

The point here is significant. If you can enable your prospect to somehow participate in the demonstration rather than just watch it, your results will often be even more outstanding.

It's why people conducting online webinars will usually ask attendees to submit answers to simple questions during their presentations. Studies have discovered that by inviting participation during the webinar, results will often be accelerated.

Let Me Take A Picture

What if a demonstration is not available?

In place of a physical demonstration, photos can help.

If I said our government is loaded with a bunch of lazy officials, maybe you'd agree, and maybe you wouldn't. But if I showed you a photo of elected officials in Congress sleeping in their seats, it would make a stronger validation of my claim, wouldn't it?

I recently noticed a photo of sleeping politicians but realized they were from the British parliament, even though it was implied they were American. When I pointed out that they were not Americans, people didn't seem to care. As one of the respondents explained, *"All politicians are the same."* That's the power of photography in helping solidify a point even if the photo isn't entirely relevant.

A major chain of convenience stores struggled because many of their outlets were getting robbed. So, someone came up with a strange idea, and almost instantly, robberies practically disappeared.

What was their solution?

They had a life-size photo of a cop placed in the stores, so they were visible from outside the front window, and almost instantly, the robberies stopped.

It was obvious the image was a photo and not a real cop. But it still worked.

So, could a photo of a cop be almost as effective as a real cop in preventing crime? Surprisingly, yes!

The Unexpected Engagement Power Of A Hand Signal

Have you ever noticed how adding a hand gesture to a slogan can increase its impact?

We all know what the raised middle-finger means. As an obscene hand gesture dating back to ancient Greece, its usage has become commonplace because it provides an easy visual of anger and contempt.

How about this?

Introduced in the 1960s by the tv show Star Trek, Mr. Spock's Vulcan hand greeting – where an open hand with the middle fingers parted to form a 'V' while saying the words, *"live long and prosper"* – has helped keep the Star Trek franchise iconic to millions of its fans.

Similarly, as I mentioned previously, Theranos founder Elizabeth Holmes introduced a hand gesture that helped her raise almost half-a-billion dollars of funding for what ultimately became a fraudulent venture.

The image of her holding a tiny vial of blood between her thumb and forefinger visualized the idea of how a single drop of blood would be able to generate an almost instant, deep analysis of a person's health.

That hand gesture proved so iconic that it emblazoned major magazine covers, helping build excitement and credibility for a technology that would ultimately never come to pass.

Still, Elizabeth Holmes demonstrated that the right hand gesture could create a simple visualization of a complex idea in a way that engages people enough to make them want to participate in the company simply by seeing the gesture itself.

During the darkest days of the Second World War, British Prime Minister Winston Churchill's two fingers forming a 'V for Victory' became a rallying symbol for those under attack and oppressed by the invading German army.

Someone else who adopted the 'V for Victory' hand gesture was author, playwright, and activist Eve Ensler, creator of the off-Broadway play, *'The Vagina Monologues.'* Although for her, the V referred to 'violence against women.'

To bring attention to her cause, she came up with a clever idea. At noon on International Woman's Day, every woman on the planet would stand up from wherever they were and show the hand gesture.

Using the power of this gesture, she was able to mobilize millions of women across the planet in a worldwide protest against the unconscionable violence towards women.

Leaders of a military coup who suspended democracy in Thailand would arrest protesters who used the 'salute-of-defiance' from the movie *'The Hunger Games'* – where protesters raised their middle three fingers. The coup leaders understood the uniting power of such a hand gesture to mobilize the masses and worked to prevent its use.

The raised fist was a unifying factor in recruiting people to the Black Panthers' cause in America in the 1960s.

More recently, although there's dispute over whether he actually raised his hands in surrender, outrage over the police shooting of black teenager Michael Brown in Ferguson, Missouri, was intensified by the rallying cry, *"Hands up, don't shoot,"* and the accompanying raised hands in surrender.

Activists have been able to expand their protests into a national movement by using the raised hands as a symbol of the mistreatment of minorities by police. They recognized that integrating a hand gesture with their slogan helped intensify the power of their protest.

In my marketing classes for the U.S. Small Business Administration, I like to explain how even experts get things wrong.

For example, I will often tell how, *"When Steve Jobs included a camera in a phone, I thought that was weird. Who needs a camera in their phone?"*

Then, tapping my forefinger to my head as if I'm about to shoot myself, I say, *"Boy, was I wrong."*

The simple act of putting my finger to my head amplifies the power of my statement.

We recognize from these examples how attaching a hand gesture to something you say could heighten its impact, adding an extra visual element that engages multiple parts of the brain.

Which is why it works so well.

How About Adding Visual 'Words' To Your Pitch

Viagra is also known as *'the little blue pill.'*

Computer and consulting giant IBM has been known as *'Big Blue.'*

Batman is also known as *'The Dark Knight.'*

Using words like these that heighten or bring attention to a visual element, even one that is not directly related to your product or idea, could heighten the impact of your message in even greater ways.

Before the Internet, *'The Yellow Pages'* was the dominant business directory. Having such a distinct visual as its name, *'yellow pages,'* made it easy to remember and engage with. Their slogan, *"Let your fingers do the walking,"* added even greater visual power to their marketing.

When Steve Jobs tried to recruit John Sculley, then president of Pepsi-Cola, to run Apple, Sculley initially refused, thinking he didn't want to work for a bunch of hippies. But, with Steve being an expert at persuasion, he knew he needed to diminish the value of Sculley's current job if he would have any chance at all of recruiting him.

Visually, what is Pepsi? Basically, it's just colored water. So, Steve whispered these fateful words to Sculley,

"You know, you can sell colored water for the rest of your life, or you can come to Apple and help me change the world."

Sculley later admitted those words gave him sleepless nights until he finally agreed to come to Apple.

That phrase may not be impactful to you or me. But the way Steve minimized Sculley's supposedly prestigious job with those simple words was enough to get Sculley to change his mind and come on board.

What Visual Comes To Mind

We often use words like these to heighten the impact of our descriptions...

snake – midget – puny – Dumbo

"He's a real snake."

"A midget truck... A midget home."

Adding words like these paints a picture that sticks in the mind, strengthening the messages we are trying to make.

When Malcolm Gladwell was writing a book about little changes that help things suddenly take off and become viral hits, he thought of the image of something struggling, struggling, struggling, inching its way uphill... until it finally passed the top and suddenly started flying downhill with ease. As he imagined the visualization of what he was describing, the words *'tipping point'* jumped out at him.

Naming his book, *'The Tipping Point,'* turned it into an instant classic, in a large part because he translated a conceptual idea into a visual that resonated with just about everyone.

Although he didn't invent the term, calling his book *'The Tipping Point'* popularized a term that had otherwise been minimally used.

Alfred Fielding and Marc Chavannes were trying to create three-dimensional plastic wallpaper with interesting little air bumps. As wallpaper, the product failed. But shippers discovered it worked incredibly well as wrapping for items to ship because of its light weight and amazing cushioning qualities, especially with fragile items.

So, what would you call a product that wraps items with tiny bubbles?

How about *'Bubble Wrap?'*

The name was so visually descriptive that it helped their product revolutionize the shipping industry.

Today, their company, Sealed Air, has become a behemoth of success, in part because of its visually descriptive name.

How Visual Words Heighten Your Prospect's Emotional Engagement

One highly effective way to gain the attention of the masses is by coming up with quotes that people are willing to share across the Internet.

Bestselling author Darynda Jones is a prime example. I remember laughing hysterically and then sharing a meme I saw with one of her quotes. It had the image of a housewife holding a gift-wrapped box, with the caption,

"I lost my virginity... but I still have the box it came in."

For a writer, when you think of *virginity*, besides sex, what's something visual that comes to mind without being raunchy?

Well, a guy might give his girlfriend or wife a present in hopes he could have sex with her. So, the gift becomes a visual that could combine with the word *virginity*, making it funny and engaging without being offensive.

"I lost my virginity... but I still have the box it came in."

I'm not sure I could have come up with such a creative choice, which probably explains why Darynda Jones is such a successful fiction author, something I could never be.

Still, reviewing quotes from someone this creative can be inspiring and might give you ideas about how you could use visuals and visually engaging text for your own product name, book title, slogan, or personal quotes.

Here are a few more of her visually engaging quotes.

"Never knock on death's door. Ring the doorbell, then run. He totally hates that."

"I chose the road less traveled. Now I'm lost."

"When I want your opinion, I'll remove the duct tape."

Funny as these quotes might be, they highlight the power of injecting visuals and visually engaging words into your slogans and attempts at persuasion.

Here are a few examples from the business world.

Let's say you work for John Deere, the tractor company. Obviously, you think of a deer running through the woods when you hear the name. That became the inspiration for their enduring logo,

"Nothing runs like a Deere."

The double entendre of a deer running and their tractors running helps their brand resonate with users.

Maxwell House Coffee created a little movie inside your head with the slogan,

"Good to the last drop."

Volkswagen crystallized the idea that their Beetle's size is a noteworthy feature, with headlines like these,

"Think small," and

"It makes your house look bigger."

For a product like Capital One credit cards, what's a visual that comes to mind? Well, let's go through the process of using a credit card and see what comes up.

First, when you're ready to pay for something, you open your wallet, pull out your card, and either slide it into a card reader, read the details to someone over the phone, or fill out the details online.

Visually, you have to open your wallet to get it out before you can enjoy the benefits.

Why not say,

"Capital One. What's in your wallet?"

As a visually heightened image, this certainly helps.

Boeing became a behemoth of the aircraft industry with the help of a simple, visually engaging power phrase.

In the early days of air travel, planes were considered unsafe and prone to crashes. To solve this, Bill Boeing created a twin-engine aircraft that was more durably constructed than conventional wooden planes and was reinforced with a metal frame. He also expanded the passenger compartment to accommodate almost a hundred passengers.

Most importantly, he included a fuel tank that could enable a flight from New York to Los Angeles in just eight hours when that same trip by train or car would take weeks.

However, with a public still fearful of air travel, he needed a slogan that would convince everyone that flying in one of his planes was as safe as driving in a car.

He could have said,

"For the first time ever, you can fly from New York to Los Angeles in just eight hours."

Instead, he applied an engaging visual with the phrase,

"For the first time ever, you can have breakfast in New York and watch the sunset in Los Angeles."

This simple phrase, elevated by the visualization of *'watching a sunset,'* is credited with having transformed air travel into a critical necessity while helping Boeing become so dominant that the federal government eventually had to step in and tell them they could make aircraft or run an airline, but they couldn't do both.

You might wonder how such a seemingly simple phrase like this could have such an incredible impact. But it did. That's the persuasive power of emotionally engaged right-brain selling.

Here's an important point. Don't be fooled by the seeming simplicity of this. Tapping the deepest emotions in your prospects can sometimes seem subtle. But it often makes the difference between moderate success and blockbuster results in ways that are surprising even to many top experts.

What's Something You'd Do Once You Own It

To create iconic ads for Porsche, they recognized that simply showing one of their cars racing down a street or on a track would make their ads look like every other sportscar promoter's. Instead, what they needed was a way to tap into the emotions engaged once someone actually owns a Porsche.

Let's say you just bought one of the most beautiful sports cars on the planet. Even after you parked it and started walking away, you'd probably be glancing back at this gorgeous piece of engineering, wouldn't you?

This became the motivation for their headline,

"If you don't look back after you park it... you have the wrong car."

As with other award-winning ads, Porsche created an iconic brand for themselves in a large part by applying visual prompts that increase the vividness of their ads.

So, what about you?

What can you add to your emails, ads, posts, and pitches that heighten your prospect's visual engagement with the product or message you're selling?

Coming up with your own sparkling, flaming words can shed the kind of streaming sunlight on your message that makes it much easier for your prospects to reach into their wallets and hand over their hard-earned cash.

>> **CAN YOU 'FEEL' THAT?** <<

Back to Steve Jobs and his introduction of iPhones to the world.

What Steve realized was, being able to run your fingers across the smooth surface of the screen as if it was a computer mouse would revolutionize the world of computing forever.

With BRAIN GLUE, we also recognize that injecting words into our conversation that refer to how things *'feel to the touch'* can also heighten the engaging power of what we say.

Words like *'slippery'* and *'slimy'* to describe a person, for example.

Mae West became an iconic figure in the world of entertainment with tactile quotes like this,

"A hard man is good to find."

M&Ms became one of the most successful candies of all time by highlighting the feel of their candies with the slogan,

"Melts in your mouth, not in your hands."

Kentucky Fried Chicken, now called KFC, became one of the largest fast-food chains in the world by focusing on the *'feel'* of their chicken pieces with the slogan,

"Finger-lickin' good."

So, what words or phrase can you add to the description of what you're selling that makes the feel of your product or idea more vivid in your prospect's mind?

>> **CAN YOU 'TASTE' THAT?** <<

We understand that describing the *delicious* taste of something could help sell it. But how about the *bad* taste of something?

Buckley's Cough Medicine became the best-selling mouthwash in Canada by focusing on its bad taste, with headlines like this,

"People swear by it. And at it."

"It tastes awful. And it works."

"Everything you want in a cough remedy. And nothing you want in taste."

"Buckley's cough syrup. Tastes like a horror. Works like a wonder."

Sour Patch Kids candies offer a tasty description of their product in their ads,

"First, they're sour, then they're sweet."

In the mid 1950s to the 1970s, R.J. Reynolds Tobacco Company marketed Winston cigarettes with the slogan,

"Winston tastes good, like a cigarette should."

Technically the phrase should have been,

"Winston tastes as good as a cigarette should."

But getting the grammar wrong didn't bother them at all. Mentioning the 'taste' of the cigarette combined with their street-wise slang helped propel it to incredible success among competing brands.

Finally, one of my favorite ads – for Nutella chocolate and hazelnut spread – has the following words scrolled in chocolate across the page, as if someone stuck their finger in the jar and wrote these words with Nutella,

"Please do not lick the page."

The point of all this is simple. Adding taste, touch, smell, sound and visual words or elements to describe your product or idea can make it easier to get people to buy it.

But don't take my word for it.

Try it for yourself. I think you'll be surprised at how adding unexpected senses to your messages will boost their vividness and emotional impact in ways you probably never expected.

Epilogue

Quick Review Of What We've Covered

Before I wrap, I'd like to share something I think will help you understand BRAIN GLUE in action. Two things, actually. They are, leveraging what you already have and the importance of getting started now rather than overthinking it.

Once you start applying just a tiny part of what I've covered in this book, as so many others have found, I believe you will be amazed at how much easier it can be to get people to buy your ideas and products.

Start By Leveraging What You Already Have

While driving to the airport recently, I passed a Beautyrest Mattress truck. Besides a good looking photo on the side, it had their slogan,

"All you feel is rested."

Now that I understand the power of BRAIN GLUE, I wonder why they used such a weak slogan when they could have leveraged their name into a much more powerful and relevant one. To me, a phrase like *"all you feel is rested"* is basically saying,

"The only thing you feel when you sleep on a Beautyrest mattress is rested."

What? You don't feel refreshed, energized, or invigorated?

To me, that slogan just seemed lame when there's a much better, more natural slogan they could have come up with that relates to the name Beautyrest.

When I hear that name, I hear two words: beauty and rest. To me, a much better slogan would be something like this,

"The most beautiful rest you will ever experience."

Doesn't that resonate and inspire you more than *"all you feel is rested?"*

Marketers sometimes overthink product names and slogans when obvious ones may be screaming out at them, if they'd just listen.

Don't let yourself fall into this trap. Instead, when coming up with a name, slogan, or power phrase, start with the obvious and work your way backwards from there. In this way, you will often uncover a power phrase that resonates more intensely and effectively with your audience.

Now That You Have Plenty Of Tools, Let's Start Using Them Right Away

Here are a few ideas to inspire you to get going with your own BRAIN GLUE names, phrases, and slogans.

USING AN ANALOGY TO HELP NEW RECRUITS UNDERSTAND THE CULTURE OF YOUR COMPANY

Let's say you're trying to recruit people, but you want applicants to understand that yours is a high-pressure company where employees are allowed to openly criticize their bosses if they feel their boss is doing something wrong.

For a new supervisor, it could sometimes feel like employees are ganging up on you to take you down, and you'd better be comfortable with that if you want to work here.

Coming up with an analogy could make this easier to understand.

How about this? Working here sometimes feels like,

"...a pack of hyenas taking down a wildebeest."

That's a memorable image, isn't it?

This is how Ray Dalio, founder of Bridgewater Associates, the world's largest hedge fund, describes his company to potential employees.

In fact, when David McCormick rose through the ranks to become co-Chief Executive Officer of the company, once he made a few mistakes, it became obvious that *"the hyenas had come after him."*

Notice how this *'hyenas'* analogy makes it easier to understand what working at Bridgewater is like?

So, what analogy or metaphor could you use to help people understand what you're proposing or offering?

USING SOMETHING 'UNEXPECTED' TO HELP CLIENTS UNDERSTAND WHAT'S MOST IMPORTANT

Let's say you're an Internet marketing company, and you want a more dramatic way to let people know their ads must appear on page one of Google. Basically, you're trying to convey the idea that,

"no one will ever find you if your ad appears on page two of Google."

What's a more memorable way to say that?

Using the *'Odd and Unexpected'* technique, you could say,

"If you want to make sure no one finds your products, we can always put your ads on page two of Google."

But let's go even further.

What's something you'd never want anyone to find? Something funny and unexpected.

How about... *'a dead body?'*

That's the process Dharmesh Shah, the founder of the HubSpot Internet marketing company went through when he came up with the phrase,

"The best place to hide a dead body is page two of Google."

Doesn't that make the point in a funny and more compelling way than simply saying, *"you need to make sure your ads appear on page one of Google?"*

Yes, it absolutely does.

USING 'PERSPECTIVE' TO SHOW HOW EASY YOUR PRODUCT IS TO USE

Let's say you're doing a magazine ad for Sure-Stick Floor Tiles. You want people to know how easy and fast it is to lay new floors in your kitchen with these tiles. How could you communicate that?

First, the words, *easy* and *fast*, are the descriptive words you want to focus on.

Starting with the word, *easy*, you could try an ANALOGY. Something like,

"Laying these tiles is as easy as making your bed."

Or you could use PERSPECTIVE by explaining how fast you can lay these tiles, with something like,

"Laying these tiles is so easy, you could do it blindfolded."

I'd create an image of a blindfolded woman standing in a kitchen on her newly installed floor to reinforce the headline.

The ad they eventually came up with focused on the word *fast* with the headline,

"It took Judy Baker longer to make a cake than to put down the floor."

The image of a woman holding a newly baked chocolate cake standing on her newly installed kitchen floor reinforced the headline and helped turn this into a successful ad for them.

See how this works?

STOP USING THE SAME OLD WORDS TO DESCRIBE YOUR OFFERING

Two important features of Timberland company's footwear and clothing products are that they're waterproof and they tend to be authentic. Meaning, if they're selling moccasins, they have been designed as traditionally as possible. If they're selling heavy-duty boots, they are the same ones that professional mountain climbers would wear.

To describe products like these, it's easy to say these products are *'waterproof and authentic.'*

The problem with a statement like that is, it's too ordinary and boring for a company trying to excite people to recognize the originality and value of their products.

Here's the clever slogan they came up with.

"They're water proven... Boots, shoes, clothing, wind, water, earth, and sky."

Rather than simply saying, *'they're waterproof,'* they used the more interesting phrase, *'water proven.'* Rather than just listing *'boots, shoes, and clothing,'* they include *'wind, water, earth and sky,'* anchoring their products to nature.

Combined with the memorable ads they created, Timberland has strengthened the value of their products and their brand by using non-conventional word combinations in their slogan and ads to exemplify the iconic nature of their products.

Is this something you could do with your own products or ideas by using uncommon words and phrases to explain them?

USING 'CHIASMUS' TO CREATE AN ICONIC IMAGE FOR YOURSELF AND YOUR BRAND

Besides offering high-value products, famed investor John Templeton built a positive reputation for himself with quotes like this,

"It's nice to be important... but it's more important to be nice."

Notice how the use of chiasmus makes the phrase more memorable than a traditional slogan or quote.

To highlight the Gordon and Betty Moore Foundation's positive mission that focuses on education, their grants director, Ignacio Estrada, used chiasmus with the phrase,

"If a child can't learn the way we teach, maybe we should teach the way they learn."

A tribute to the enduring power of chiasmus, Greek philosopher Plato created 'sticky' quotes like this,

"Wise men speak because they have something to say; fools because they have to say something."

I'm not sure your own BRAIN GLUE generated phrases will last 2,000 years as Plato's have, but done properly, they will trigger the kinds of heightened emotional engagement that will make whatever you say stand out from the crowd, giving you an advantage in the battle to pierce the mind of your prospects.

USING A 'METAPHOR' TO MAKE YOUR BUSINESS STAND OUT FROM THE CROWD

When Gregg Curtis opened a gym for kids based on the famous Cirque Du Soliel theatrical programs, rather than giving it a conventional name, he used the metaphoric, *'Airealistic Circus and Flying School,'* – a name that sets a unique and vivid expectation in the minds of kids and parents.

With such a unique name and concept, it has become one of the hottest places to enroll your kids in Southern California, with a never-ending waiting list to get in and with businesspeople constantly approaching him, trying to get him to franchise his concept.

USING TOOLS LIKE 'SENSE ELEVATION,' 'ALLITERATION' AND 'EXPECTATION' TO NAME YOUR PRODUCT AND BUSINESS

How about the successful kids' animated dancing movie, *'Happy Feet,'* – using 'sense elevation's' visual anchor, focusing on feet, combined with the emotional word, *happy*.

How about a comedy store using alliteration, maybe calling it something like, *'Larry's Leaky Laughs?' or 'Gags–N-Giggles.'*

How about adding visual or tactile words to make a name or phrase 'stickier,' like these...

The Dark Side,

The Bright Side,

Fasten your seatbelts; it's going to be a bumpy night,

Squatty Potty,

Dunkin' Donuts.

Or unusual combinations like these,

The Beasty Boys

Screamin' Demons

The Big Short

Little Big Man

Let's say you were starting a bakery, and your name was John Johnson. You might want to name it *'John's Bakery'* or *'Johnson's Bakery.'* But a better idea might be considering the power of a BRAIN GLUE-based alliterative or rhyming name, like,

'Big Bob's Bakery,' or

'Bake-N-Take.'

Or perhaps you could set an expectation of greatness with,

'The Most Incredible Bakery This Side of the Planet.'

Maybe these are crazy ideas, and you could do even better.

But remember this.

Whenever you apply behavioral techniques like these that engage multiple parts of your prospect's brain, your ability to influence, persuade, and sell easier and faster can skyrocket in ways that will often surprise you, as it has for the thousands of professionals who have already tried this with their own products, services, book titles, posts, ads, and ideas.

Of course, having a power name or slogan is not all that's needed to achieve the success you truly desire. You still need a good product or idea.

But there are plenty of people with great products and ideas that never get to enjoy the level of success they could, simply because the first impression they give is not as engaging as it could be.

Remember John Gray earlier in this book. As he told me, an incredibly simple change of his book title and concept, from *'Men and Women in Relationships'* to *'Men Are From Mars, Women Are From Venus,'* was all he needed to transform his modestly selling book into a blockbuster.

So, what about you? Are you sitting on an incredible product or idea that isn't getting the traction you hoped for?

If the answer is yes, I invite you to go through the techniques in this book again to discover for yourself how to alter your logically awesome offering into an emotionally engaging super-offering.

By doing this, I believe the success you experience will catapult you to a level that exceeds your greatest expectations.

Conclusion

I've covered a lot in this book. I've taken you through how BRAIN GLUE amplifies your message by making your ideas 'sticky,' so they stick in your prospect's brain like glue, making your words, products, and book titles easier to sell.

I used the acronym STEAM ATTRACTORS to cover the fourteen elements you can use to apply BRAIN GLUE to your own products and ideas.

These include...

- Setting the Right Expectation
- Tribal Alignment
- Easing Their Understanding
- Analogies and Metaphors
- Anchoring to Something They Already Know
- Toning Your Voice So It's More Persuasive
- Triggering Oxytocin Brain Chemicals
- Rhyming Your Way to Persuasion
- Alliteration as a Persuasion Power-Tool
- Chiasmus as an Unexpected Persuasion Tool
- Trigger-Words to Use and Avoid
- Odd and Unexpected Mental Surprises

- Rejection as a Way to Attract, and
- Sense Elevating as a Way to Heighten a Person's Mental Engagement

Because persuasion itself is one of the most valuable skills you will ever use, learning and understanding how BRAIN GLUE works could be one of the most important skills you ever develop.

The good news is, all it takes is one or two of these tools to change your life.

Remember, a simple toilet stool became massively successful with the help of a clever name, *'Squatty Potty.'*

Carey Smith renamed his company *'Big Ass Fans,'* and that helped propel his business to a level of success even he could never have imagined.

Attorney Johnny Cochran used rhyme and street talk to create a simple phrase – *"If the glove don't fit, you must acquit"* – that helped him win the trial of the century and skyrocket his career to the top of one of the most competitive industries on the planet.

So, how about you?

If you're serious about accelerating your ability to influence, persuade, and sell just about anyone easier and faster than you've ever done it before, remember, BRAIN GLUE is definitely the best place to start.

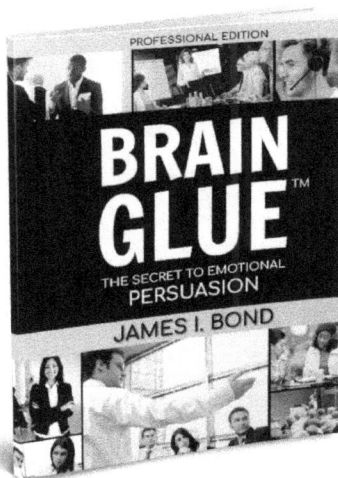

Please Leave a 1-Click Review

(It makes a huge difference!)

If you enjoyed this book,
I would be incredibly thankful if you take just 60 seconds to write a brief review on Amazon,
even if it's just a few sentences.

Thank you!

Endnotes

Preface

Redintegration: American Psychological Association – Dictionary of Psychology – "APA Dictionary of Psychology". dictionary.apa.o rg. Retrieved 2019-11-21, https://dictionary.apa.org/redintegration -

National Library of Medicine, Cognitive Psychology, 2005 Mar;50(2):133-58. doi: 10.1016/j.cogpsych.2004.07.001. Epub 2004 Dec 2.

Shark Tank's 5 most successful products – South China Morning Post, by Leah Thompson, May 15, 2021 - https://www.scmp.com/magazines/style/celebrity/article/3133512/shark-tanks-5-most-successful-products-ranked-daymond

Chapter 1

Buckleys: The Good Taste of Bad Taste, Brand Autopsy, by John Moore, November 2007 - https://brandautopsy.com/2007/11/buckleys-the-go.htmlChapter 3

The Big Interview With Dan Rather – Interview with Edward Norton, AXS TV, February 27, 2014 / October 20, 2020

Chapter 2

Carbonite: How Limbaugh's Gaffe Tainted Unwitting Brands, Inc Magazine by Erik Sherman, March 5, 2012

- https://www.inc.com/velocity-global/why-investors-are-looking-at-your-hr-practices.html

Carbonite and Howard Stern: Legal Insurrection, by William A. Jackson, March 16, 2012 - https://legalinsurrection.com/2012/03/carbonite-and-howard-stern/

Anita Roddick: Our Fight Never Stops – The Body Shop, https://www.thebodyshop.com/en-ca/about-us/activism/our-activist-heritage/a/a00081

Body Shop Boss Goes Back to the Rainforest, The Guardian, by Sarah Butler, February 13, 2016 - https://www.theguardian.com/business/2016/feb/13/body-shop-boss-back-to-rainforest-jeremy-schwartz-anita-roddick

Chapter 3

The Inventor: Out for Blood in Silicon Valley – The Elizabeth Holmes Story, HBO, by Alex Gibney, March 18, 2019 - https://www.imdb.com/title/tt8488126/

Startup: A Silicon Valley Adventure, by Jerry Kaplan, Penguin Books, 1994

50 years ago: Roy Disney made Walt's dream come true, Click Orlando, by Ken Pilcher, October 1, 2021 - https://www.clickorlando.com/theme-parks/2021/10/01/50-years-ago-roy-disney-made-walts-dream-come-true/

Summary: Secrets of Closing the Sale, by Zig Ziglar, May 18, 2020 - https://waiyancan.com/summary-secrets-of-closing-the-sale/

50 Facts That Should Change The World 2.0, MJF Books, by Jessica Williams, 2007

Made to Stick: Why Some Ideas Survive and Others Die, Random House, by Chip Heath and Dan Heath, 2007

Jaws in Space: Powerful Pitching for Film and TV Screenwriters, Kamera Books, by Charles Harris, 2016

'Breaking Bad' Creator Vince Gilligan Reflects On Meth And Morals, NPR, by Terry Gross/Fresh Air, October 11, 2019 - https://www.npr.org/2019/10/11/769312766/breaking-bad-creator-vince-gilligan-reflects-on-meth-and-morals

How Mexico Claimed the Tourist Crown, Bloomberg Businessweek, by Maya Averbuch and Rafael Gayol, May 16, 2022

In a World of Supply Chain Blocks-Adaptation, Bloomberg Businessweek, Edited by James E. Ellis, February 21, 2022

Chapter 4

Gorilla Glue/From the bench: Woodworker to entrepreneur, and back again, Fine Woodworking, by Mark Singer, 2021 issue – https://www.finewoodworking.com/2020/11/05/from-the-bench-woodworker-to-entrepreneur-and-back-again

Naked Juice: Grocery.com, 2021 - https://www.grocery.com/naked-juice/

Swedish Poetry: Water Proved, Bloomberg BusinessWeek, by Chelsea Kyle, April 11, 2011

When It Rains, It Pours: The History Of The Morton Salt Girl, History Daily, by Karen Harris - https://historydaily.org/history-morton-salt-girl-umbrella

Carbon Capture Comes of Age, Bloomberg Businessweek, by Akshat Rathi and Stephan Nicola, May 9, 2022

Warren Buffett quotes - https://www.goodreads.com/author/quotes/756.Warren_Buffett

HuffPost, Dr. Maya Angelou: 'Be A Rainbow In Somebody Else's Cloud' By Lisa Capretto, May. 30, 2014 – https://www.huffpost.com/entry/maya-angelou-oprah-rainbow_n_5413544

Manscaped: Meet Paul Tran, Founder and CEO of Rocketship DTC Brand MANSCAPED™, Business Wire, April 13, 2021 - https://www.businesswire.com/news/home/20210413005280/en/Meet-Paul-Tran-Founder-and-CEO-of-Rocketship-DTC-Brand-MANSCAPED%E2%84%A2

FlingGolf, A New Spin On The Sport, Sees Booming Sales After 'Shark Tank' Appearance, Forbes, by Mike Dojc, August 9, 2021

Shark Tank – Season 12, ABC TV, FlingGolf, May 14, 2021

Chapter 5

Read the full text of Ukrainian president Volodymyr Zelenskyy's speech to the US Congress, Quartz, by Hasit Shah, March 16, 2022 – https://qz.com/2142992/transcript-of-volodymyr-zelenskyys-speech-to-the-us-congress/

Dunkin' Donuts: The Food that Built America, The History Channel, March 13, 2022

The Origin Of Nasty Gal's Name Is Genius, Romper, by Carralynn Lippo, April 21, 2017 - https://www.romper.com/p/is-nasty-gal-really-named-after-a-song-netflixs-girlboss-depicts-the-companys-beginnings-52181

Tootsie Roll to Footzyrolls: See ya in court, CNN Money, By Parija Kavilanz, November 18, 2011 - https://money.cnn.com/2011/11/18/smallbusiness/tootsie_roll_footzy_roll/index.htm

NFL Super Bowl/Superball, The Toys that Built America, The History Channel, 2022

The Story of the George Foreman Grill, Foreman Grill Recipes - https://foremangrillrecipes.com/the-story/

How Ryan Reynolds and Mint Mobile worked without becoming the joke, Tech Crunch, by Jordan Crook, Brian Heater, November 28, 2020 - https://techcrunch.com/2020/11/28/how-ryan-reynolds-and-mint-mobile-worked-without-becoming-the-joke/

How the Impossible Burger is changing the debate over GMO foods, CNBC, by Sully Barrett, February 13, 2020, - https://www.cnbc.com/2020/02/13/how-the-impossible-burger-is-changing-the-debate-over-gmo-foods.html

Buyout Giants Rebrand as Forces for Good While Seeking Profits, Bloomberg Businessweek, by Sabrina Willmer, November 4, 2021 - https://www.bloomberg.com/news/articles/2021-11-04/private-equity-funds-embrace-esg-for-good-while-seeking-profits

Positioning, The Battle for Your Mind, McGraw Hill, by Al Ries and Jack Trout, 1981

Chapter 6

How To Convey Power With Your Voice, Forbes, by Susan Adams, November 25, 2014

- https://www.forbes.com/sites/susanadams/2014/11/25/how-to-convey-power-with-your-voice/?sh=25988ee282e7

The Inventor: Out for Blood in Silicon Valley – The Elizabeth Holmes Story, HBO, by Alex Gibney, March 18, 2019 - https://www.imdb.com/title/tt8488126/

Chapter 7

The two faces of oxytocin, American Psychological Association, by Tori DeAngelis, February 2008 - https://www.apa.org/monitor/feb08/oxytocin

Using Laughter To Build Trust At Work, Forbes, by Brian M. Harmon, PhD, April 10, 2019 - https://www.forbes.com/sites/forbescoachescouncil/2019/04/10/using-laughter-to-build-trust-at-work/?sh=5ab6335343c9

Reagan recovers in second debate, Politico, by Andrew Glass, October 21, 2018 - https://www.politico.com/story/2018/10/21/this-day-in-politics-oct-21-1984-910774

Chapter 8

Standin' on the Corner Park, RoadsideAmerica.com - https://www.roadsideamerica.com/story/12603

Wonder Bread, The Food That Built America, The History Channel, 2022

Chapter 9

How Lady Gaga Got Her Name and Why She Doesn't Use Her Real One, Good Housekeeping/GH.com, by Kayla Keegan, January 7, 2019 - https://www.goodhousekeeping.com/life/entertainment/a25737162/how-did-lady-gaga-get-her-name/

The Donut Revolution, The Fast History of, History Channel, May 8, 2022

Chapter 10

Antimetabole Definition, Literary Devices - https://literarydevices.net/antimetabole/

Chapter 12

Regina Rhymes With, Great Canadian Bucket List, by Robin Esrock, April 15, 2015 - https://www.canadianbucketlist.com/regina-rhymes-with-fun/

Regina rhymes with more words than fun, Regina Leader-Post, by D.C. Fraser, February 11, 2016 - https://leaderpost.com/news/local-news/regina-rhymes-with-more-words-than-fun

Mommy Needs Vodka, Facebook - https://www.facebook.com/mommyneedsvodkablog

How Clint Eastwood Landed His Man With No Name Role, Screen Rant, by Nicholas Raymond, March 6, 2022 - https://screenrant.com/clint-eastwood-man-no-name-cast-part-story/

When Moviegoers Started Watching Films From the Beginning, Hollywood Reporter, by Thomas Doherty, October 12, 2020 - https://www.hollywoodreporter.com/news/general-news/when-moviegoers-started-watching-films-from-the-beginning-guest-column-4075683/

KISS – Keep It Simple, Salesperson, Nightingale Conant Corp., by Fred Herman with Earl Nightingale, 1982

Tested Sentences That Sell, by Elmer Wheeler, Prentice-Hall, Inc., 1937

Lou Wasserman - The Original Man in Black, Los Angeles Times, by Valli Herman-Cohen, June 7, 2002 - https://www.latimes.com/archives/la-xpm-2002-jun-07-lv-agent7-story.html

Is the World Ready for Freakonomics Again, Time, by Justin Fox, October 26, 2009 - https://content.time.com/time/subscriber/article/0,33009,1930520,00.html

Reuben Mattus, 81, the Founder of Haagen-Dazs, The New York Times, by Richard D. Lyons, January 29, 1994 - https://www.nytimes.com/1994/01/29/obituaries/reuben-mattus-81-the-founder-of-haagen-dazs.html

A Hundred Monkeys, Bloomberg Businessweek, by Kalle Oskari Mattila, April 18, 2022

Waiter, There's A Rat in My Soup - and It's Delicious, The Wall Street Journal, May 31, 1991 - http://www.mit.edu/people/dmredish/wwwMLRF/links/Humor/Rat_Restaurant.html

Why this major brand's name was called "dyslexic cheekiness," CBC Radio, by Terry O'Reilly, May 16, 2019 - https://www.cbc.ca/radio/undertheinfluence/why-this-major-brand-s-name-was-called-dyslexic-cheekiness-1.5138226

Grow Like You Mean It, Inc., by Carey Smith, September, 2021

Chapter 13

You Ask, We Answer: 'Parental Advisory' Labels — The Criteria And The History, NPR, by Tom Cole, October 29, 2010 - https://www.npr.org/sections/therecord/2010/10/29/130905176/you-ask-we-answer-parental-advisory---why-when-how

Wizard of Lies: Bernie Madoff and the Death of Trust, St. Martin's Griffin, by Diana B. Henriques, May 16, 2017

Chapter 14

Dirty Love, The American Scholar, by David Lehman, June 20, 2017 - https://theamericanscholar.org/dirty-love/

Lavender for Anxiety: The Best Way to Use This Calming Herb, Healthline, by Marnie Vilall, - https://www.healthline.com/health/anxiety/lavender-for-anxiety

Scent of Coffee on Seoul Buses: What's the Marketing Secret, CNBC, by Brian Tam, August 15, 2012 - https://www.cnbc.com/2012/08/15/scent-of-coffee-on-seoul-buses-whats-the-marketing-secret.html

Folklore.org: It Sure Is Great To Get Out Of That Bag! – http://www.folklore.org/StoryView.py?story=Intro_Demo.txt

KISS – Keep It Simple, Salesperson, Nightingale Conant Corp., by Fred Herman with Earl Nightingale, 1982

The Inventor: Out for Blood in Silicon Valley – The Elizabeth Holmes Story, HBO, by Alex Gibney, March 18, 2019 - https://www.imdb.com/title/tt8488126/

Thai Protestors Adopt 'Hunger Games' Salute As Symbol of Defiance, The Hollywood Reporter, by Abid Rahman, October 20, 2020 - https://www.hollywoodreporter.com/news/general-news/thai-protestors-adopt-hunger-games-salute-as-symbol-of-defiance-4080290/

'Hands Up, Don't Shoot' Didn't Happen in Ferguson, Washington Post, by Michelle Ye Hee Lee, March 19, 2015 - https://www.washingtonpost.com/news/fact-checker/wp/2015/03/19/hands-up-dont-shoot-did-not-happen-in-ferguson/

Steve Jobs: The Exclusive Biography, Simon & Schuster, by Walter Isaacson, 2011

The Accidental Invention of Bubble Wrap, Smithsonian Magazine, by David Kindy, January 23, 2019 - https://www.smithsonianmag.com/innovation/accidental-invention-bubble-wrap-180971325/

Darynda Jones Quotes - https://www.goodreads.com/author/quotes/4175419.Darynda_Jones

Boeing, The Machines That Built America, History Channel, 2021

Buckleys: The Good Taste of Bad Taste, Brand Autopsy, by John Moore, November 2007 - https://brandautopsy.com/2007/11/buckleys-the-go.htmlChapter 3

Epilog

Bridgewater Associates: Be The Hyena. Attack The Wildebeest, Dealmaker.com, by Bess Levin, May 10, 2010 - https://dealbreaker.com/2010/05/bridgewater-associates-be-the-hyena-attack-the-wildebeest

About The Author

James I. Bond is one of America's leading behavioral management and business marketing specialists.

For thirteen years he ran one of Southern California's leading behavioral management firms, working with a who's who of American business.

Early in his career, he ran an advertising agency in Montreal, working with a wide range of Fortune 500 and smaller firms.

He is a past workshop chairman for the resource partner of the U.S. Small Business Administration, has been a featured guest speaker at three Southern California universities, and has been a popular guest on a wide range of marketing and business podcasts.

James resides in Thousand Oaks, California.

www.ingramcontent.com/pod-product-compliance
Lightning Source LLC
Chambersburg PA
CBHW021431180326
41458CB00001B/224
* 9 7 8 0 9 9 8 8 6 5 7 4 4 *